LIVE ALL
YOU CAN

·················· ⚾ ··················

BY JAY MARTIN

BIOGRAPHIES
Nathanael West: The Art of His Life (1970)
Always Merry and Bright: A Biography of Henry Miller (1978)
The Education of John Dewey (2003)

LITERARY CRITICISM
Conrad Aiken: A Life of His Art (1962)
Robert Lowell (1970)

LITERARY HISTORY
Harvests of Change: American Literature, 1865–1914 (1967)

PSYCHOANALYSIS
Who Am I This Time? Uncovering the Fictive Personality (1988)

FICTION
Baseball Magic (2008)

AUTOBIOGRAPHY
Winter Dreams: An American in Moscow (1979)
Journey To Heavenly Mountain (2002)

DRAMA
William Faulkner: A Question of Place (1980)
Trial Days in Coyoacan (2001)

SOCIAL CRITICISM
Swallowing Tigers Whole: Conceptions of the Desirable in
American Life and Education (1997)

LIMITED EDITIONS
A Corresponding Leap of Love: Henry Miller Living and Dying (1996)
Henry Miller's Dream Song (1996)

EDITED
Winfield Townley Scott (1962)
Critical Essays on "The Waste Land" (1968)
Twentieth-Century Views of Nathanael West (1972)
A Singer in the Dawn: Reinterpretations of Paul Laurence Dunbar (1975)
The Dunbar Reader (1975)
Mexican Folk Tales (1977)
Paul Laurence Dunbar: Uncollected Works (2000)

LIVE ALL
YOU CAN

ALEXANDER JOY CARTWRIGHT AND
THE INVENTION OF MODERN BASEBALL

JAY MARTIN

Columbia University Press   New York

Columbia University Press

Publishers Since 1893

New York   Chichester, West Sussex

Copyright © 2009 Columbia University Press

All rights reserved

Library of Congress Cataloging-in-Publication Data

Martin, Jay.

Live all you can : Alexander Joy Cartwright and the invention of modern baseball /

Jay Martin.

p. cm.

Includes bibliographical references and index.

ISBN 978-0-231-14794-1 (cloth : alk. paper)

ISBN 978-0-231-51969-4 (e-book)

1. Cartwright, Alexander Joy, 1820–1892. 2. Baseball—United States—Biography.

3. Baseball—United States—History. I. Title

GV865.C32M37   2008

796.357092—dc22

[B]   2008053267

Columbia University Press books are printed on permanent and durable acid-free paper.

This book is printed on paper with recycled content.

Printed in the United States of America

c 10 9 8 7 6 5 4 3 2 1

References to Internet Web sites (URLs) were accurate at the time of writing. Neither the
author nor Columbia University Press is responsible for URLs that may have expired or
changed since the manuscript was prepared.

"Live all you can; it's a mistake not to. It doesn't so much matter what you do in particular, so long as you have your life. If you haven't had that what have you had? . . . What one loses one loses; make no mistake about that. . . . [One] lives, in fine, as one can. Still, one has the illusion of freedom; therefore don't be, like me, without the memory of that illusion. I was either, at the right time, too stupid or too intelligent to have it; I don't quite know which."

—Henry James, *The Ambassadors* (1903)

. . . .

To Helen

—*that first night at Naupaka*

CONTENTS

LIVE ALL
YOU CAN

··················· ⚾ ···················

THE BIRTH OF THE FATHER

Alexander Joy Cartwright Jr. was inaugurated into the Baseball Hall of Fame in Cooperstown, New York, in 1938. The citation on his bronze plaque reads boldly: "ALEXANDER JOY CARTWRIGHT, JR. 'FATHER OF MODERN BASEBALL.' SET BASES 90 FEET APART. ESTABLISHED 9 INNINGS AS A GAME AND 9 PLAYERS AS TEAM. ORGANIZED THE KNICKERBOCKER BASEBALL CLUB OF N.Y. IN 1845. CARRIED BASEBALL TO PACIFIC COAST AND HAWAII IN PIONEER DAYS." From the immense number of kinds of ball games regulated by a chaos of different rules, Cartwright assembled a single game that was so well thought through, so simple to grasp in its essentials, and so American in its character that it has endured for more than a century and a half on the foundation he established and has spread to the rest of the world. He was born in New York City on April 17, 1820, and died in Honolulu on July 12, 1892, and my biography tells his complete story for the first time.

But before I narrate a full account of Cartwright's life it is important to notice where he came from. Like the rest of us, he did not "father" himself. He was the issue of a family, a family history, and family traditions. He participated in the creation of an "American character" and type in the way he conducted his life. To understand the evolution of baseball we need to see where he came from, since he too was the issue of a long evolution.

Whatever mechanical activity of Cartwright's ancestors in England established the family name is lost in history. By the time we can locate them historically they had become seafarers. Soon they would also become Americans. At the age of twenty-one, Edward Cartwright emigrated from England to New England in America around 1661, a little over thirty years after the arrival of the Puritan colonists in Massachusetts Bay. In his case, commercial considerations seem to have predominated over spiritual ones. He and his forebears came from Dittisham in Devonshire, where fishing had immemorially been the major occupation of the village. He came to the American continent to fish the rich banks lying off New England's shores. Sailing out of Hog Island, near Portsmouth, he harvested the fishing grounds around the Isle of Shoals, but he also fished as far north as Prince Edward Island and as far south as Block Island. On land, he achieved a sufficiently high esteem that he was appointed constable, but he had his own share of boisterous behavior. He was censured for "allowing his pigs to run at large on the common," and fined for "drunkenness, assault, disturbing the peace, selling rum, and for controversies with Indian neighbors."

Before 1665, Edward met and married Elizabeth Morris of Roxbury. In 1666, Elizabeth gave birth to a boy, whom they named Nicolas. Other children followed, including Edward Jr. During these years, the many islands off New England's coast were rapidly developing their own ports for fishing. Nantucket was one of these. Invited to teach fishing in Nantucket, Edward moved his family there in 1676.

Edward's descendents flourished in Nantucket. Later Cartwrights would continue in his steps to be seafarers and sea captains, manning and commanding traders and whaling ships, fishing vessels, and ships to transport immigrants and fortune seekers to America's shores. Edward Jr. married Ruth West of Martha's Vineyard, and together they produced several children, all with appropriate Old Testament names, such as Judah, Gideon, and Samuel. The first Cartwright to be named "Alexander Joy" was born in Nantucket around 1784. "Joy" was the name of a prosperous Nantucket family. Reuben Joy, for instance, was one of the twenty Nantucketers who served under the command of John Paul Jones on the *Ranger* and the *Bon Homme Richard* during the Revolutionary War. The Cartwright and Joy families were closely related. Somewhere in the Cartwright genealogy a son married a daughter of the Joy family. We also know that Obed Joy, a well-known Nantucket shipmaster, married an Anna Cartwright, and that they named their second son Alexander Cartwright Joy. Like his father and most of the Cartwrights and Joys before him, this Alexander Joy was raised to follow the sea.

President Thomas Jefferson's Embargo Act of 1804 crippled New England shipping by cutting off all commerce between New England, England, and France. Many once-thriving ports in New England were wrecked economically. In Salem, where tall-masted ships were lashed rotting to the wharf, there were bread lines, and soup kitchens were opened to feed the destitute. The situation in Nantucket was perhaps even more desperate. On April 30, 1812, some of the prominent citizens of Nantucket met to draft a letter to Congress petitioning for aid. Alexander Cartwright, George Cartwright, and four Joy brothers, including Reuben Joy, signed a petition predicting that without congressional assistance, "we shall be destitute of fuel and provisions and our families must be reduced to the extremes of hunger and want."

When America resumed foreign commerce in 1815, following the end of the hostilities, New England shipping had been so reduced that a large part of the international shipping trade now went instead to New York City, which possessed one of the finest harbors in the world. It had the advantage, too, which the New England islands and ports did not have, of easy access to transportation inland, where the push of settlers westward was beginning. The Erie Canal had been built, and the rivers of New York made connection with the West possible. Many stubbornly resolute residents of Nantucket continued on the island with hope for a renewed prosperity that never really came, but the more energetic and farseeing of the islanders understood that New York held the future for foreign commerce. These were part of the migration southward to New York.

Still unmarried at the age of thirty-two, partly because of his involvement in the war, the straitened circumstances of Nantucket, and his confinement on a British prison ship, Alexander Joy Cartwright finally decided to make the move to New York. On earlier sailing and trading ventures he had docked in the port of New York several times. Anyone could see that the city was alive with commercial activity, that a spirit of forward-going hustle and bustle was apparent there, and that Manhattan Island had natural beauties that rivaled or even surpassed its pleasing commercial prospects. In variety and scenic beauties it far surpassed Nantucket. The island was full of flowers, fields, meadows, scenic cliffs and prospects, rivers and streams. It was so famous for the fragrance of its flowers, and not just at the "Bowery," that European travelers remarked that the sweet airs of Manhattan signaled the near approach to the port even before the seafarer could see the shore. Jasper Danckaerts said that in its purity, agreeableness, and fineness, the air of Manhattan was the best in the world. In vivid contrast to his lean years in Nantucket, for Alexander, New York was a land of plenty. Every kind of food was available, game was plentiful; the city's oyster beds were world famous; fruits and vegetables were piled up in the markets. Both the clink of money and the natural climate of New York suited Alexander, and he settled in the city in 1816. Now he was ready, like his ancestor Edward, to start in a new place and to make his own family. He courted, and on December 3, 1816, married Ester Rebecca Burlock. Early in their marriage, as New York grew rapidly and new homes were erected, the married couple moved from the corner of Grand and Roosevelt Streets on the Lower East Side, to 364 Water Street, adjacent to the docks; then, in 1818, to Lombardy Street. In this house, on April 20, 1820, his son and namesake, Alexander Joy Cartwright Jr., was born. He was the second of seven children.

Alexander Sr. seemed always to be in a frenzy to move, and he soon moved again. In 1821, he relocated to 13 Rivington Street, near the Bowery. Here he lived until his son and namesake was in his seventh year. Then Alexander Sr. picked up once again and moved everyone to Cherry Street, with a view over the East River to Brooklyn. By this time, Manhattan was expanding north, and the Cartwrights followed its flow. Early in the 1830s, they moved up to Mott Street.

By now Alexander Sr. had fathered three sons and four daughters, including Benjamin, Charles, Catherine, and Esther. He had prospered in shipping ventures for nearly two decades. Now he was partner in the shipping firm of Cartwright and Grant, located at 5 Frankfort Street. He was fifty-two years old. But economic disaster lay ahead. The economy of the United States was unregulated and heavily influenced by frenzied speculation, which periodically, about every five to seven years, ended in recession or depression. As financial speculation mounted once again in the mid-1830s, Captain Cartwright plunged into the market at nearly the very moment when its bottom dropped out. By 1837, the panic became the largest in American history until the 1929 Depression. In New York alone, a hundred million dollars evaporated overnight. Two hundred and fifty businesses closed. Cartwright and Grant was one of them. The family was ruined. They slid down the ladder of success, all the way back to Rivington Street, which they had risen from fifteen years before. Alexander Joy Cartwright Jr. was sixteen years old.

It was time for him to go to work. By 1836 and 1837 lower New York was already on its way to becoming a tangle of office buildings. As the panic reached its peak and subsided, shrewd business investors could see that stocks had precipitously fallen too far and funds were severely undervalued. Stockbrokers, many of whose clients had been ruined a few months earlier, were now hiring again. Alexander Jr., whom everyone called "Alick," was taken on as a clerk by Coit and Cochrane, stock brokers. It was a thoroughly respectable and solid firm, Levi Coit, the senior partner, having been long established in New

York business circles. Alick did the usual things that all clerks did—filing, copying, and running errands.

His father tried to revive his shipping business but no longer had the energy or ready capital for it, and he settled for a salaried job as an inspector for the Marine Insurance Company. This helped, along with the contributions that the boys were now making, and he began to climb out of Rivington Street again. Within a year the family moved to 305 Brown Street. No further climb upward in neighborhoods occurred, and there he remained as marine inspector, now for the American Mutual Insurance Company, until he retired in 1847 at the age of sixty-three. Then he moved north, at the frontier of the city's uptown growth, to Twenty-fourth Street. By the time he died, his whole estate was worth $11,913.20. In the meantime, his children were maturing and leaving home. Alick accepted a job as teller in the Union Bank on Wall Street. At first he went to live with his older brother Benjamin, who was rising to be a cashier in City Bank, New York's most prestigious banking firm. Alick, for his part, was sufficiently confident of his future that at the age of twenty-two he proposed marriage to Eliza Ann Gerrits Van Wie, the daughter of Pieter Gerrits Van Wie and his Irish wife, Mary Walsh. The Van Wie family had long been chiefly associated with Albany, New York, where they had large landholdings. But Pieter had found more entertainment in New York City than in rural upstate. Once married, he was decidedly not entertained by marriage or childrearing. An intimate friend of Martin Van Buren, then the great power-to-be in New York state politics, Pieter was a dandy like his friend. Family legend had it that the two of them got into several scrapes and were "pinched once or twice" for boisterous behavior. Pieter seems to have abandoned his wife and child not long after the birth. Raised by her uncle Robinson in New York City, Eliza had the Van Wie name but none of its money.

Still, following their wedding day on the first Saturday in June 1842, with a ceremony in the Third Free Presyterian Church located on Thompson and Houston Streets, Alick and his bride moved to an excellent neighborhood at Eighth Street in an area then known as Clinton Place, after the illustrious New York governor. Coincidentally, one of Alick's best friends, Peter DeWitt, was distantly related to DeWitt Clinton, and when Alick's first son was born eleven months after his marriage, on May 3, 1843, he and Eliza named the boy DeWitt Robinson, after Alick's friend and baseball teammate and Eliza's uncle. The place of birth given for the baby boy was 11 St. Mark's Place, the residence of the distinguished attorney Peter DeWitt Sr., father of Cartwright's best friend, Peter Jr. Two years later, Eliza gave birth to a daughter, Mary.

Even before the birth of Mary Groesbeck Cartwright on June 1, 1845, the cyclical business economy of the United States was sliding into another economically shallow period. Alick's job at Union Bank had seemed to be secure and to hold prospects of slow advancement until he might eventually reach the elevated position of "chief cashier," roughly equivalent to today's CFO. The classical Union Bank building, which the depositor entered between stately, solid Corinthian columns, seemed a guarantee of perpetuity. But in the Wall Street fire of 1845, the Union Bank building was burned beyond repair, along with 213 other buildings on Wall Street. This blaze put Alick out of work and bankrupted his father's Merchant Marine Insurance Company, and he too, at the age sixty-one, now had to find employment. Alick was also forced to relocate to reduce expenses, first moving to 558 Fourth Street, then to 4 Stone Street, and at last to 341 Sixth Street, not far from his parents. In September 1845 he and his little family lived on Fourth Street between Avenues C and D, over on the east side, near the dry docks on the East River.

Alick's younger brother Alfred de Forest was also out of work. The two of them—in partnership with Henderson Green and perhaps with a little family assistance—cobbled together enough cash and credit to open a stationery and book store. This was located first at 67 Wall Street until, when a better location offered, they moved closer to the head of Wall Street, in sight of Trinity Church, then renowned for its tall spire. New York City had 200,000 inhabitants, and the literacy rate was high among the city's business class. Such a shop as theirs, wisely located, had a fair prospect of success. Nearby was Wiley's bookstore, where avid readers might see James Fenimore Cooper, William Cullen Bryant, or J. K. Paulding scanning the shelves for new arrivals. Very likely, they visited Cartwright's shop as well. Edgar Allan Poe would also certainly have been an early visitor to the Green and Cartwright store, since the offices of the *New York Evening Journal*, which Poe edited, were directly across the street from their shop. New York was already producing a literature to rival New England's, one that was more secular, cosmopolitan, and westward-looking. And the city promised to continue to develop new authors. Herman Melville, for instance, published his first four novels between 1846 and 1849, while the doors of the Cartwright store remained open.

Alick worked as a stationer. But he was a dreamer, and he dreamed another dream.

THE DREAM

· · · · · · · · · · · · · · · · · ·

Alexander Joy Cartwright Jr.'s dream was baseball. Like most boys and many girls in New York, Alick had grown up playing the varieties of ball games then current in the city. For young men, ball games were one of the city's chief entertainments in its mild weather from April through October. During summer, the extended hours of daylight allowed for games in the twilight after work. On the weekends, the entire day was at the disposal of the players, when games and family picnics could be combined. During the 1830s, ball games came to be organized into teams that revolved around civic organizations. Among these in New York were the various volunteer fire engine companies organized to fight frequent blazes. In a crowded city that had a large number of combustible wooden buildings, fire was an ever-present danger. The premier firefighting company was Oceana Hose Co. no. 36, which was reorganized in 1845 by Alick's brother Benjamin, who later became the first fire commissioner of New York City. Another fire company was Knickerbocker Engine Co. no. 12. Its engine and firefighting equipment were housed below Murray Hill, near Sunfish Pond, which the men used as their water source when they helped to fight the great House of Refuge fire of 1838. At this time, firefighting was done by volunteer assemblies. It was a public-spirited activity, though, to be sure, a large number of the volunteers sold fire insurance and thus had a special interest in firefighting. The presence of numerous fire companies created intense competition between the most able and agreeable young men. And this, in turn, led to considerable attention to the decorative splendor of the companies' costumes and pumping engines. The firemen splashily attired themselves in red shirts, high-crowned hats, black pantaloons, and heavy boots. At the first signal, they would rush to their engine house and wheel out their grand pumper, glistening with fresh paint and gleaming metals, and dash to the latest conflagration. Meanwhile, admiring and cheering crowds gathered to watch the incendiary battle.

To promote their activities and to finance the purchase of equipment, the fire companies marched in holiday parades and devised firemen's balls, contests, and award ceremonies. Naturally, too, members of individual companies of volunteers formed social relations in their neighborhoods. Just as naturally, the young men in them formed sports clubs. They rode horses or fished together, and, of course, they played ball games. Depending on the number of men present, they played versions of the traditional town-ball, one o' cat, or cricket with one another. At the earliest time, there was still no thought of competition on the field between fire companies or other organizations. Matches were club events, played by choosing sides among members. Engine Co. no. 12 had about forty members. About half of them showed up for any one game—plenty to make opposing sides.

We know that in the early 1840s, Alick and Alfred joined the Knickerbocker Engine Co. no. 12 and that in 1842 they and their fellow volunteers were playing "base-ball" wherever they could find a field in Manhattan. The lowest reaches of the island were beginning to be rather built up, but they still found plenty of expansive fields or vacant lots. There was a fine spot at Twenty-seventh Street, where the first Madison Square Gardens was later to be built. Sections of the parade ground that stretched west from Lexington Avenue between Twenty-third and Thirty-fourth Streets provided lots of open space. Forty-seventh and Fourth, where the first depot of the Harlem River Railroad was eventually built, was another good spot. So was the open meadow next to Sunfish Pond. Fields suitable for base-ball games were also likely to have a fine tavern nearby for conviviality. Social and family relations were an integral accompaniment of the game; part of the fun was in searching for fresh places of social festivity and athletic prowess.

By 1845, fire companies began to think of extending their competition in fighting fire to competition on the ball field. Alick was a leader on his team. At six feet, two inches, and 210 pounds, he was one of the strongest hitters and also a first-rate pitcher. Now he took the lead in organizing the team and the game it played. On September 13, 1845, he and Alfred were leading members of a team which they naturally named the "Knickerbockers Base Ball Club" after their fire company. Alex was the vice president and secretary of the club. In addition to the Cartwright brothers, the original organizers of the Knickerbockers were William R. Wheaton—a lawyer—Duncan F. Curry, Ebenezer R. Dupignac Jr.,

W. H. Tucker, and Jacob H. Anthony, an assistant cashier at the Bank of the State of New York. They were soon joined by Peter DeWitt, Abraham Tucker, Colonel James Lee, Dr. Franklin Ransom, James Fisher, and William Vail. Daniel Adams later recalled that the members of the club were "merchants, lawyers, Union Bank clerks, insurance clerks, and others who were at liberty after 3 o'clock in the afternoon." Many years later, in 1887, William Wheaton claimed that he had first codified baseball: "it was found necessary to reduce the rules of the new game to writing. This work fell to my hands, and the code I then formulated is substantially what is used today." Probably Wheaton, a Knickerbocker player, did assist in the discussion of an earlier set of rules or a later revision of the rules in 1848, but clearly it was Cartwright who put pen to paper and initially "formulated" them in 1845. For his team, Cartwright drew up a constitution, and the members agreed upon the by-laws which he recommended. In 1877, Duncan F. Curry stated definitely: "Baseball is an American game and owes its origin to Mr. Alexander J. Cartwright.... Well do I remember the afternoon when Alex Cartwright came up to the ball field with a new scheme for playing ball." He continues:

The sun shone beautifully, never do I remember noting its beams fall with a more sweet and mellow radiance than on that particular Spring day. For several years it had been our habit to casually assemble on a plot of land where the Harlem Railroad Depot afterward stood. We would take our bats and balls and play any sort of game. We had no particular name for it. Sometimes we batted the ball to one another or sometimes played one o' cat.

On this afternoon I have already mentioned, Cartwright came to the field—the march of improvement had driven us further north and we located on a piece of property on the slope of Murray Hill, between the railroad cut and Third avenue—with his plans drawn up on a paper. He had arranged for two nines, the ins and outs. That is, while one set of players were taking their turn at bat the other side was placed in their respective positions on the field. He had laid out a diamond-shaped field, with canvas bags filled with sand or sawdust for bases at three of the points and an iron plate for the home base. He had arranged for a catcher, a pitcher, three basemen, a short fielder, and three outfielders. His plan met with much good natured derision, but he was so persistent in having us try his new game that we finally consented more to humor him than with any thought of it becoming a reality.

At that time none of us had any experience in that style of play and as there were no rules for playing the game, we had to do the best we could under the circumstances, aided by Cartwright's judgment. The man who could pitch the speediest ball with the most accuracy was the one selected to do the pitching. But I am getting ahead of my story. When we saw what a great game Cartwright had given us, and as his suggestion for forming a club to play it met with our approval, we set about it to organize a club.

Curry's statement was supported by a famous early baseball player, George Wright, who wrote, "In the Spring of 1845, Mr. Alex J. Cartwright, who had become an enthusiast in the game, one day upon the field proposed a regular organization" of the Knickerbockers' game. Cartwright wrote the rules down in a little five-inch by three-and-a-half-inch black book that he took from his stationery shop. On the cover in gold letters, he stamped "Knickerbockers." Dues for players were set at five dollars per year. Dressed in the newly fashioned team uniform of straw bowlers, sporty flannel shirts and vests, blue pantaloons and jackets, six of the organizers went to have their photo taken. Alfred and Alick draped their arms around each other in the back row, and one of the sitting players stuck a cigar in his mouth at a rakish angle, mugging for the camera.

The Knickerbocker charter put stress upon the social character of ballplaying and the social status of ballplayers. Article V emphasized that members of the team should be held to high standards of personal behavior. Players, it stated, should not use "profane or improper" language. Were any caught doing so, a fine of six and a quarter cents could be levied for each infraction. Improperly disputing with an umpire could cause the basic fine to be doubled. Abuse of the team captain would bring an immense fifty-cent penalty. Baseballers were to be American gentleman. No wonder that the baseball historian Harold Seymour referred to Cartwright's Knickerbockers as a "social club with a distinctly exclusive flavor."

The club rules were formed. The team was named. All that remained was to state precisely what rules of play would prevail if games among Knickerbockers and eventually against other teams were to be and mean anything but fun and frolic. After all, if it was to be a gentleman's game, and not just the rowdy pastime of English and American children, it would have to be regulated and organized. As the early baseball historian William Cauldwell noted in 1905, the boys' game before 1845 "had no regular form or shape . . . until the formation of the Knickerbockers Club, when boys of a larger growth took the matter in hand." Baseball was henceforth to be a regulated and refined game. Baseball, no less than American social life, was to be guided by the rule of law and Victorian etiquette.

Alexander Joy Cartwright Jr. invented baseball in 1845. This was an age of invention, and Cartwright became one of its great inventors. Base-ball, rounders, and town-ball retreated into the past. A new, distinctively American game was assembled. It did not derive from the traditions of Europe but rather was invented through the practical, enlightened thinking that had created the union of the United States, whereby uniform national laws became standard everywhere and at every time. The quest in America for a national identity had extended from its roots in revolutionary politics and social egalitarianism to a national capitol and a national flag and a national bird and national arts. Now it went all the way to baseball as the national game.

Baseball meant bases. Cartwright designated that a "base" would not be a stake or a rock merely meant to mark progress around the field to home but a place where the runner could stand—a flat base. This made the next step possible, as Cartwright went about designing baseball as an engineer designs a machine, as Fulton designed the steamboat *Clermont* in 1807 or Eli Whitney the cotton gin. The parts had to fall together. With bases it became possible to eliminate the most strained and unruly part of the game—"plugging" a runner with the ball to make him out. Now, if the ball arrived at first base before the runner, he was "out." He didn't have to be hit with the ball. This meant, too, that at the other bases a runner could be "forced out." The outlawing of plugging a runner to make him out also allowed the ball to become harder and allowed hits for much greater distances. We still have balls used by the Knickerbockers. These weigh about ten and a half ounces and have a rubber center that was wrapped in yarn, then covered in leather. With a harder ball, the pitcher had to be moved further than a few feet from the batter to prevent injury. Cartwright moved the pitcher to forty-five feet from home plate. At that distance, then, the gentle underhand toss to the batter's favorite spot would no longer be possible. The pitcher had to throw fast, in an effort to make the batter strike out. At first pitches were thrown underhand with a stiff arm, but eventually it was inevitable that overhand delivery would become common. Then the pitcher could be moved still further from the batter. With a faster pitch, strikeouts would become more frequent. Cartwright designated that three strikes would make an out. But in the constitutional spirit of checks and balances, he also created the "walk," obliging the pitcher to deliver the ball over the plate, or else "walk" the batter to first. The bats used by the Knickerbockers measured two and a quarter inches in diameter and could be any length and weight.

But how was the field to be designed? The rectangular field of play in round-ers or the multidirectional field of cricket allowed batters to hit in all directions, sometimes far from the bases, so that the new concept of force-outs wouldn't work easily. And the variable distances between home and first, first and second, second and third, and third and home, initially gave advantage to the runner and then to the fielders as the batter attempted to round third and make home. This was not symmetrical, ordered. Cartwright solved these two problems at once by making the field of play square, turning it ninety degrees to make a diamond, and demanding that "fair" balls must be hit forward within the extension of the lines of the diamond into the outfield. Years later, Cart-wright reminded Charles Deborst that the first diamond-shaped field was on "the pleasant field of Hoboken in New Jersey, the Elysian Fields, . . . where . . . most of the early games were played." Indeed, according to Frank Borsky, it was Cartwright himself who laid out the first baseball diamond at Elysian Fields. But how far apart should these bases be? Here, more than in any other decision, Cartwright showed off his inventiveness, in accord with the scientif-ic, mechanical focus of his time. If the bases were placed, say, sixty feet apart, the runner would have an immense advantage. He would almost always beat a throw. Contrariwise, if the base paths were a hundred and twenty feet from one to another, few runners would arrive safely. Cartwright studied the actual activities in a ball game so as to achieve equality of advantage between runners and fielders. At ninety feet (or thirty paces) between bases, the ball and the runner would arrive at nearly the same time. Ninety feet it would be.

In 1947, Alick's grandson, Bruce Cartwright Jr. spoke to a journalist about his early memories:

> When I was a small boy it was my great joy to hear grandpa tell about the early days of baseball in New York. . . . Grandpa, having an inventive mind, decided to improve [town-ball] . . . by framing rules, including the defini-tions and dimensions of the playing field.
>
> So, one day Alex and his team-mates decided to lay out a diamond. First, he placed a piece of wooden board to represent "home," then walked thirty paces [at 3 feet per pace] toward first base, designating the point with a sand bag. For each succeeding base he stepped off another thirty paces in a line at a right angle to the preceding one, thus forming a square. . . .

"You know," said Mr. [Bruce] Cartwright with modest pride, it is one hundred years since the first regular game was played by the Knickerbockers . . . but the size of the original diamond has remained unchanged."

In town-ball or rounders, the side would not be "out" until the entire team of players had batted. This made for a slow game, but Americans adored speed. Cartwright designated three "outs" as retiring the side. Victory in many earlier ball games was achieved by the first team to reach twenty-one runs, on the condition that both teams had had equal turns at bat. But with a mere three outs required to retire a side, and with force-outs and strikeouts, many hours might be required before any team would reach twenty-one. With the logic of mathematical deduction, Cartwright determined that three outs would make an "inning" (when one team was "in") and three or more innings would constitute a game, whatever the score. The same mathematical precision came to apply to the number of players. With the field of play confined to the enclosure of the "foul lines," fewer players were needed to cover the field. Cartwright reduced the two catchers behind the plate in town-ball to one, since batters could not hit fair balls backward. With three infield bases to be covered, he placed one fielder at each base. The many players who previously stood helter-skelter behind the infielders were eliminated and reduced to three outfielders, similar to the three infielders. Then Cartwright (or perhaps Adams with Cartwright) inserted a "shortstop" who could roam between infield bases and relay throws from the outfield. (We know that Daniel Lucius Adams played shortstop in the first recorded game.) Cartwright counted these positions and, with the pitcher included, arrived at the magic number of nine players.

Just over three weeks after the Knickerbockers drew up their by-laws and rules, they played the first game under the new regulations on October 6, 1845. From his stationer's shop Cartwright brought along a new scorebook in which the games could be recorded with regard to "Names," "Hands Out," "Runs," and "Remarks." Places for the date and name of the umpire were also designated. After all, with the new rules making much more intricate play, the umpire increased in importance. If the batter was like the president and the fielders like the Congress, the umpire was the Supreme Court. In Cartwright's famous rules the umpire was so described: "All disputes and differences relative to the game, to be decided by the Umpire, from which there is no appeal." Fines were levied freely for protesting the umpire's "calls." Cartwright himself got a double fine of twelve cents in October for too vigorously "disputing the umpire." In his own hand Cartwright recorded the results of this first game.

That Cartwright was the team's best hitter is clearly signaled by the scorebook, for he was the first batter to come to the plate in this first display of modern baseball. After all the preparations made for the new game, this first moment was anticlimactic. Cartwright made an out. One down. James Moncrief batted next. Two outs. Peter DeWitt came to the plate. Out. The side was retired in order. The opposing side came up. Duncan Curry made an out. Then, finally, Fraley Neibuhr made the first hit under modern baseball rules. Maltby followed with another hit. The next batter, Dupignac, was out, but Turney and Clare both reached base before Gourlie made the third out to end the first inning.

Cartwright's team caught life in the second. Tucker, Birney, and Moorhead all reached base, while Smith made the first out. Then Cartwright and Moncrief failed again.

Curry's team came up. Niebuhr got a second straight hit and so did Maltby. Dupignac hit safely. Then Turney made the first out. Clare and Gourlie made hits. This brought Curry up, but he failed to reach base. Niehbuhr and Maltby both hit safely, and so did Clare. Then Curry made the third out.

Cartwright's team started well in the top of the third inning, with hits by DeWitt and Tucker before Smith again made the first out. Moorhead followed with an out. Cartwright came to bat and finally made his first hit. Moncrief also got on base for the first time. So did DeWitt, Tucker, Smith and Birney, but Moorhead made his second out of the inning and the rally was crushed.

The end of the third inning would bring the game to a close. Neibuhr was finally stopped. Out number one. Maltby, Dupignac, and Turney hit safely before Clare made the second out. Gourlie followed and reached base. So did Curry—finally—and Neibuhr. But Maltby ended the game.

At the end of three innings the runs scored by the players stood as follows:

Cartwright	1	Curry	2
Moncrief	1	Niebuhr	3
DeWitt	2	Maltby	1
Tucker	3	Dupignac	2
Smith	0	Turney	2
Birney	0	Clare	0
Moorhead	1	Gourlie	1
Total	8	Total	11

After both sides had batted three times, this first practice game was called. Curry's team had scored eleven runs, while Cartwright, though the "Father of Baseball," led the first losing team, with a total of eight runners reaching home. Alick contributed one hit and one run. (However, in a later game recorded in the scorebook, Cartwright, batting second, redeemed his reputation by having a perfect day at the plate and leading his team in runs scored with five. His team won that day, twenty-eight to twenty-seven.) To be sure, not all the new rules were adhered to in the first intrasquad game. Only fourteen players arrived at the Elysian Fields, near Hoboken, New Jersey, so seven players made each side.

In the fall of 1845, New York had an Indian summer. The weather stayed fair, and with their woolen uniforms the Knickerbockers were able to play every Thursday or Friday afternoon between October 6 and October 18, with eighteen or more players showing up for subsequent games. All the statistics were duly recorded by Cartwright in his scorebook. From the first, baseball was closely associated with accounting and records. Primarily the Knickerbockers games were played by sides chosen from members of the club. One historian conjectured that "they strived to be sole proprietors of the new sport."

"A friendly match of the time-honored game of Base was played at Elysian Fields," on October 21, 1845, the *New York News* reported. Baseball was expanding rapidly. Other independent teams were being formed. It appears that on this occasion Cartwright's New York Knickerbockers were challenged to a "friendly match" by a team of Brooklynites. Cartwright's team won twenty-four to four, aided by the first recorded "grand slam," a "four aces" home run with the bases loaded. Still, Brooklyn was not willing to concede preeminence in baseball to New York, and the *News* reported that "two more Base clubs are already formed in our sister city Brooklyn, and the coming season may witness some extra sport." Indeed, the paper reported that the Brooklyn team had already agreed to a rematch with the Knickerbockers on October 24 and that this game would be decided by the team that achieved "the first 21 aces or runs." One of the Knickerbocker players, E. A. Ebbets, had close associations with Brooklyn and was a relative of the man who would later found Ebbets Field.

After the Knickerbockers had played fourteen recorded games during the fall of 1845, cold weather brought a recess. But as soon as warm weather returned, on April 10, 1846, the beginning of the Easter holiday, the Knickerbockers resumed play. Cartwright headed his scorebook grandly with the date and the notation "Commencement of the *Season*." The score on opening day was

forty to thirty-five. By June 19, the Knickerbockers had played seventeen practice games among themselves. Alick's brother, Alfred de Forest Cartwright,
played in and umpired some games. So did his brother-in-law (married to
Kate), George D. Cassio. Now they were ready to form what was to become the
next moment in the expansion of baseball.

Two separate teams were to play each other, the Knickerbockers against the
"New York Nine." At the head of the scorebook, a Knickerbocker player titled
it the "1st Match Game," featuring the "Knickerbocker Baseball Club" versus
"New York." Certainly, it was not the first match game, for that had been played
the previous season against a Brooklyn team. But it is the first match game for
which we have a scorecard, the first historically documented game between
two somewhat distinct teams. According to one contemporaneous observer,
this historic match game was "played under perfect skies as lady visitors sat
under a canvas pavilion to protect their alabaster complexions from the sun."
It was played at Elysian Fields. Duncan F. Curry described this "first" match
game on June 19:

> "Well do I remember that game," continued Mr. Curry, the first regular game
> of baseball ever played hereabouts, and the New Yorks won it by a score of
> 23 to 1. An awful beating you would say at our own game, but, you see, the
> majority of the New York Club's players were cricketers, and clever ones at
> that game, and their batting was the feature of their work. The chief trouble
> was that we had held our opponents too cheaply and few of us had practiced
> prior to the contest, thinking that we knew more about the game than they
> did. It was not without misgivings that some of the members looked for-
> ward to this match, but we pooh-poohed at their apprehensions, and would
> not believe it possible that we could lose. When the day finally came, the
> weather was everything that could be desired, but intensely warm, [and]
> yet there was quite a gathering of friends of the two clubs present to witness
> the match. The pitcher of the New York nine was a cricket bowler of some
> note, and while one could use only the straight arm delivery he could pitch
> an awfully speedy ball. The game was in a crude state. No balls were called
> on the pitcher and that was a great advantage to him, and when he did get
> them over the plate they came in so fast our batsmen could not see them."

Jerry R. Erikson has reproduced the "Diagram" of the baseball field made
by Alexander Cartwright in late 1845 and regularly introduced for practice ses-

sions in the spring of 1846. This was the field for the first recorded match game. Erikson writes:

> Players voted in favor of it, and the playing field for the first game between organized clubs was marked off according to this diagram, with the pitching distance at 45 feet. . . . Since then the only changes in arrangement by Cartwright are that shortstop now plays back of the baseline, catcher plays closer to the plate, positions of umpire and scorer have shifted, and plate has been moved back into the corner of the triangle.

The final score of this "match game" was twenty-three to one. Internal evidence suggests, however, that the New York Nine team consisted of sometime Knickerbocker players. The scorebook actually first listed the "New York" players under K.B.C. (Knickerbocker Baseball Club), then someone crossed this out and designated the team as "New York." Players who had been in previous lineups at Elysian Fields games, such as William Tucker, Daniel Adams, and Jacob Anthony, were in the lineup under "Knickerbocker Baseball Club," while Doctor Franklin Ransom, an original Knickerbocker and a member of the medical society of New York, was in the lineup for New York. The "1st Match Game," it appears, was between the original Knickerbockers who stayed in New York to play and those who now made Elysian Fields their "home." Cartwright umpired this game and fined the Wall Street broker James Whyte Davis a nominal six cents for swearing at him after a disputed call.

This game is part of history as well as legend. It has been certified in the law. In 1972, in writing the Supreme Court majority holding in *Flood v. Kuhn* (407 U.S. 258), Associate Justice Harry Blackmun began the opinion of the Court: "It is a century and a quarter since the New York Nine defeated the Knickerbocers 23-1 on Hoboken's Elysian Fields, June 19, 1846, with Alexander Jay [sic] Cartwright as the instigator and the umpire. The teams were amateur, but the contest marked a significant date in baseball's beginnings. That early game led ultimately to the development of professional baseball and its tightly organized structure." Blackmun termed baseball "the 'national pastime.'"

Elysian Fields had several advantages. First, it was located on the New Jersey side of the Hudson River, with such scenic beauty that it was here that the "Hudson River School" of painters flourished, the first important group of artists depicting America's natural wonders. Second, it was easy to get there. The players would walk together down to the ferry terminal at Barclay Street and pay thirteen cents for a round-trip fare on the Stevens Hoboken Ferry. Once on the Jersey side, a short walk from the terminal following the river up Hudson Street brought them to a broad field surrounded by undergrowth and woods on three sides and, on the cleared side, taverns, such as the McCarty Hotel, where it is recorded that the team ate, once buying thirty dinners at $1.50 each. Many New York residents took Colonel John Stevens's ferry over to this resort area to spend a day in the open. The players had a built-in audience of picnickers here, along with drinking establishments where they might quench their thirst or get a bite to eat. Elysian Fields was, as William A. Mann writes, "one of the most popular outdoor recreational places in the New York metropolitan area. It was a perfect site for ball games." Sometimes refreshments were delayed until the players had crossed back to the Manhattan side after the conclusion of a game. In the Fijux Hotel, near the Barclay Street ferry, at number 11 Barclay, the Knickerbockers would sometimes continue the day's fun, review their individual efforts, and debate the progress of the new game, all the while choosing and sampling further refreshments.

In Cartwright's scorebook a record was kept in his own hand as to his personal performance from 1845, when the Knickerbockers were organized, to his departure from New York for the West. He recorded that he played in 121 games, scored 448 runs, and was retired 354 times.

Club teams, rules, enthusiastic and partisan fans, an open grassy meadow, a "home field," the excitement of the competition, the summer sun, eating snacks and drinking beer . . . the national game of baseball had been born. In 1846 a perceptive New York journalist named Walt Whitman noticed baseball. Very likely he had seen Cartwright play. He wrote: "I see great things in baseball. It is our game—the American game. It will take our people out-of-doors, fill them with oxygen, give them a larger physical stoicism. Tend to relieve us of being a nervous, dyspeptic set. Repair those losses and be a blessing to us." Ten years later Whitman would publish the first edition of *Leaves of Grass* and begin to reinvent himself as America's national poet. But in 1846 he saw at the very outset what was already destined to be the national sport, Cartwright's invention. On several later occasions Whitman spoke of the healthy physical development that baseball playing could bring, reflecting the insistence in Cartwright's charter and by-laws for the Knickerbocker team that they sought "the attainment of healthful recreation" in baseball.

Cartwright and his Knickerbocker teammates came at a dramatic time in the history of the burgeoning new nation. In the early nineteenth century, the calls to fashion a distinctive American culture were heard everywhere in the land. Americans had proved themselves powerful enough to defeat England for a second time in the War of 1812. Europe—*old* Europe—as many people were saying, had been left behind, abandoned. Waves of immigrants were departing from its ports daily to flock to American shores. The United States was a new presence on the world stage. To its citizens a unique epoch in world history was being inaugurated in North America, and therefore everything about Americans should be different. Most Americans and such transplanted Europeans as Crevecoeur believed that this new character should be manifested everywhere. In this spirit, John Montgomery Ward, himself a star player for the New York Giants, later wrote in his book *Base-ball: How to Be a Player*, that baseball was the athletic equivalent of the American democratic system of government, for while "it has doubtless been affected by foreign associations, it is nonetheless distinctively our own."

Americans in the early republic relished multiplicity, variety, novelty, difference, experiment, invention. Equally, they cherished the rule of law. Both were embodied in their newly adopted federal Constitution. At the end of the 1830s, base-ball exemplified the first tendency. It had nearly an unending multiplicity. It was indeterminate, always new, an experiment in what would work. It was like the frontier, a daily invention, lawless. It might have stayed that way—and in some sense, it has. Stickball, with a pink rubber "spaldeen" or a tennis ball and a strike zone chalked upon a wall; "whiffle ball"; tennis-racquet ball, using city street sewers as markers; balls pitched and slapped with an open hand— these are some of the descendents of the unregulated variety of the ball games existing in 1830s and 1840s. But with adult teams forming, challenges made, and championships to be determined, some sort of rule of common law would be needed, unless ball was destined to remain a pick-up game played mostly by children. Madison, Hamilton, and Jay had ably defended a Constitution that could apply uniformly to the thirteen states. But no equivalent constitution had yet appeared to turn base-ball into baseball. A new, national political system had been invented on native shores. A distinctive American literature was being shaped in the 1830s and 1840s by Emerson, Cooper, Poe, Irving, Hawthorne, and Melville. A national bank had been created. Crevecoeur, James Fenimore Cooper, George Bancroft, and many other commentators were claiming that in America a "new man" was being fashioned. Sports of all kinds were thriving everywhere, but no distinctive national sport had emerged. The American landscape, with its extensive open spaces, seemed likely to make ball games the best candidate for a national sport. What other country in the world so proliferated with such a plentitude of untouched land open to the public—commons, meadows, plains—fields of dreams?

"Elysian Fields"—the very name spoke of dreams. There, in 1845 Alexander Joy Cartwright Jr. laid out a field and stamped rules upon it. Decades later this particular field was paved over by modern progress, but the game remained and grew until it was played nearly everywhere in the world

The first grand sign of its universality came when baseball was brought around the world by Spalding's tour in 1888 and 1889. Many foreign journalists commented positively on the muscular development and the speed of the players, but most of all, they noticed the Americanness of the game. The nation had a national sport that would in time bid to be an international one, just like the nation in which it flourished.

CARTWRIGHT, DREAMING AGAIN

Everything seemed to be happening at once in the United States. The news that gold had been discovered in California in 1848 spread rapidly across the country. From the first announcement in the San Francisco papers to the appearance of the story in papers stretching from New York to Honolulu, the excitement over the momentous discovery spread with amazing rapidity. New Yorkers like Cartwright first heard of the gold strikes on August 19, 1848, when the *New York Herald* printed a letter claiming that prospectors were making thirty dollars a day. The discovery of gold in California was announced even earlier in Hawaii by the Honolulu *Polynesian* on June 24, 1848, and caused a good deal of excitement among Honolulu entrepreneurs.

Back in New York, despite the gold fever, for Cartwright baseball's development remained the burning issue. With the help of Adams and Wheaton, Cartwright made a final revision of his rules, under which the Knickerbockers would play until the team went out of existence.

Meanwhile, Cartwright's stationery store had plenty of competition and was not as profitable as he had hoped. Bookselling was badly organized in the United States, and distribution was to remain haphazard until the end of the century. Alick, Alfred, several of the Knickerbockers, and many of their friends and colleagues in business saw a golden opportunity beckoning from the California mining fields. Announcements of gold strikes resulted in intense conversations among the men about the prospect of "striking it rich" in the West. And finally conversation turned into compelling fantasies, and then fantasies turned into plans. Simply, several of Alick's friends had been infected by the "gold bug" and resolved to seek their fortunes in California. Alfred DeWitt, brother of Alick's best friend, Peter DeWitt, was the first to start. He left New

York for San Francisco on April 6, 1848, aboard the *Belfast*. Peter himself arrived in California on May 1850. The first of the actual Knickerbockers team to depart for California was Frank Turk. After a journey through Mexico, he traveled by sea on the U.S. cutter *Edith* to San Francisco, arriving on May 29, 1849. He had been appointed assistant postmaster of San Francisco, and he opened a law practice by July 10, 1849. William Wheaton arrived in San Francisco on August 30, 1849. The New York Knickerbocker players were starting to reassemble in the West.

While California seemed to be offering gold and wealth for the asking, New York City was experiencing one of its periodic downturns in 1848 and 1849. Both of the brothers set out for California in early 1849.

Two ways to travel to California existed. One was to go by foot and wagon across the country, along the Santa Fe, Oregon, and California trails. The other was to take a sailing vessel south along the coast of the Americas, where at various ports food and other necessities could be replenished, then to round Cape Horn and sail north to San Francisco. Both routes had evident dangers. Resupply was difficult on the overland route, Indian raids were reported, and the fear of the Rocky Mountains and Great American Desert was based in reality. Ships, on the other hand, were subject to the vicissitudes of storms, reefs, long periods of calm, and dependence upon unpredictable captains and crews. A small party on the overland route could strike out on their own. The passengers on a sailing vessel were hostages to chance even more than those who traveled the overland route. But if all went well, the ship might be faster and safer.

Alick decided to proceed overland. His brother Alfred chose to board the brig *Pacifico*, a Peruvian vessel that had been trading along the east coast of the United States and was homeward bound on January 23, 1849. Alick had not so much as gotten a passport by the time Alfred left, and so he started much later. On February 23, 1849, a passport was issued to Alick, signed by Secretary of State James Buchanan. Cartwright was certified "a citizen of the United States," and those whom he might contact were importuned "to give him lawful aid and protection" "in case of need." In lieu of a photo, Alex's passport described him as six feet, one inch tall, with a medium forehead, black eyes, large nose, medium mouth, round chin, black hair, dark complexion, and oval face. While Alfred was already at sea, Alick waited in the city until this passport arrived.

Alfred made a bad choice. Food was in short supply on his vessel from the beginning. Six of the passengers died from scurvy, and the rest were near starvation. By the time the *Pacifico* reached Rio de Janeiro the passengers brought charges against the captain before the American Consul there. This was, indeed, a case of the need for "lawful aid and protection" guaranteed to U.S. citizens by their government. The American and British consuls joined together to hold the ship in port until an investigation could be completed. In due course, the claims of the passengers were upheld and the captain was removed. Later, the *Pacifico* remained in its Peruvian homeport for an extended period. The exhausted travelers finally arrived in San Francisco on August 5, 1849, 194 days after leaving Rhode Island.

Though perhaps more arduous, Alick's overland journey proved to be less hazardous and thirty-eight days shorter. Taking a ledger from his stationery store, Alick kept a journal for a large part of his journey. In it he indicates that most of the 156 days he took to travel across the country he went on foot, though sometimes on horseback, and—during periods of dysentery—prone in a wagon.

On March 1, 1849, a mere eight days after his passport was issued, Alexander Joy Cartwright Jr. bid his friends, family, and fellow Knickerbockers farewell. When he left his wife, Eliza, he did not know that she was two months pregnant with their third child, a girl, who was eventually born on October 5, 1849, and named Catherine Lee after Alick's favorite sister, Catherine, and one of his best friends on the Knickerbockers, Colonel James Lee. We know the exact date of his departure because years later, when Cartwright was informed by Louis Lucy, secretary of the Honorable Society of California Pioneers, that he had been elected a member, he sent in his dues of $110 and added: "Left New York March 1st 1849 and crossed the Plains—arrived in California July 1849."

Accompanied by a few friends among twenty other men, Alick headed for the gold fields. His trip across the country began briskly, in the modern mode. The initial stages of the journey west were planned by President D'Arcy of the Camden and Amboy Railroad, who traveled with the company as far west as Pittsburgh. The long and difficult trip began on familiar grounds at the Cortland Street terminal in lower Manhattan, where the pioneers boarded a ferry for Newark. At Newark railroad station Alick paid four dollars for travel toward Philadelphia on the morning's 7:30 A.M. express steam-car of the New Jersey Railroad, one of several independent but connecting lines. He changed cars at New Brunswick and then at Trenton, transferring to the Trenton and Philadelphia Railroad. By the end of the first long day, Cartwright and his companions arrived at the Walnut Street Wharf Station in Philadelphia. After an overnight stay at the cost of eleven dollars, Cartwright and the others proceeded by rail to Pittsburgh, arriving slightly over twenty-four hours later. At Pittsburgh, Cartwright purchased an outfit for the ensuing trip. He also arranged to join a wagon train led by the famous guide Colonel William Henry Russell. His purchases were shipped separately to Independence, Missouri, where the overland journey would commence from Russell's nearby camp. In the meantime, Cartwright traveled to St. Louis by the National Road, passing through Ohio, Indiana, and Illinois.

In 1849, St. Louis was a city at the margin of the frontier. There, settlers from the East were opening businesses. Prairie scouts and Indians mingled with them, and prospectors heading for California were getting outfitted for their big strike. These citizens were accompanied, of course, by the usual assortment of criminals, con men, prostitutes, and speculators. According to his grandson, Bruce Cartwright Jr., in St. Louis Alexander saw "mountain men in their buckskin suits with fringes and fur caps," carrying powder horns and Kentucky rifles, next to "ladies in the latest Paris gowns." Gambling halls, saloons, and brothels were located close by thriving businesses that shipped western produce and foods to the East, and brought eastern supplies to the West.

At St. Louis, Cartwright boarded a steamboat to Independence, where the Santa Fe trail started, and where Colonel Russell, who was to guide his train, waited. Cartwright had chosen his leader wisely. Among the numerous guides and wagon masters who took adventurers west, Russell had a distinguished past and was a reliable leader. He was one of the most famous wagon masters and guides on the Oregon Trail, and one of the earliest train leaders in opening the California trail in 1848 and 1849. In *The Oregon Trail*, Francis Parkman gives an account of his first meeting with Russell, quaintly describing him as "drunk as a pigeon" at Fort Bernard, near Fort Laramie. (Parkman probably mistook Russell's case of mountain fever for drunkenness.) Russell was born in Kentucky, practiced law in Nicholas County, and was elected to the state legislature in 1830. In 1831, he moved to Missouri. Henry Clay became his mentor. He served in the Black Hawk War (1832) and was a U.S. marshall from 1841 through 1846. In the provisional government of California under Frémont, he was secretary of state. From 1847 through 1849 he led trains of up to 150 wagons. It appears that his trip west leading Cartwright's train was his last journey, since after arriving in San Francisco with Cartwright, he moved to San Jose, California, and practiced law there for the next twelve years.

Russell assembled his train outside Independence in Boundary Line camp, where thirty-two wagons and 110 men slowly gathered together. Russell organized, trained them in handling wagons, and checked the travelers' supplies. During the week of preparation, they had serious chores to do but found time, Cartwright wrote, for hunting and fishing, swimming and playing "Base-ball." Russell outlined his proposed route to them, and they fixed wagon covers, securely stowed their possessions, and made acquaintance with the other travelers, for each would have to depend on the others if the wagon train were to complete its journey successfully. On the April 23, members of the various wagon trains consolidated by Russell met in a council and agreed to strike out for the "gold diggings" of California along the Santa Fe Trail until they reached the Oregon Trail. They would follow that to South Pass and then north of the Salt Lake in the territory of the Utes, and finally go on the California Trail through the Sierra Nevada Mountains to the "golden state." On Tuesday, April 24, 1849, the weather was clear and warm at seven A.M. They started on the long journey. A trip of 101 days still stretched before him, until Cartwright would arrive at Fort Sutter on July 4, 1849. And even then his travels would not end.

Cartwright went across the plains three years after Parkman made his journey. Upon its first publication in 1849, Parkman's book was originally titled *The California and Oregon Trail* to exploit the recent gold rush fever of 1848 and 1849. However, Parkman never set foot on the California Trail, and the final title is the accurate one. By contrast, Cartwright's was among the earliest gold-seeking trains to transit the California Trail, which had been extended from the Oregon Trail in the late 1840s. So, Cartwright's journal represents that of the gold rush pioneers, extending Parkman's account. The journal that he kept is revelatory of the man's humor, compassion, and perseverance.

C artwright began his journey on April 24, 1849. On the first day, he walked twenty-three miles. He was exhilarated by the beginning of the great adventure, and despite long, arduous, sometimes dangerous days to come, his enthusiasm was to continue. Each day he pushed a little further into the unknown continent. Civilization had stopped at St. Louis. Mixing with his excitement were apprehension and loneliness. Everything was new. The gold seekers had to learn how to survive on the trail, in an unsettled country. They were learning to deal with novelty. Besides, whatever their professions and education had been, here they were equal in their new adventure. In this democracy of newness, only character would count.

Alick had character—and a fine, literary manner. The style of his journal possesses the virtues of his age, a period when Walter Scott's, Washington Irving's, and James Fenimore Cooper's remarkable talents for description, especially of nature, were on full display and became a staple of American narratives of the 1840s and 1850s. Depictions of the grandeur of America's nature by the Hudson River School of painters and, later, by painters traveling in the West, paralleled the word pictures of writers and made Americans highly attentive to their natural surroundings. Though he left school at sixteen—actually rather late for many boys of his time—Cartwright's experience in selling books and his passion for poetry gave him an awareness of literary trends that flowed smoothly into his writing. His journal is full of several vivid, extended descriptions of nature and man, the "grand" or sublime views of scenery, and the wonders of human excellence. He actually named the main influences on his style when he noted that there was such wild grandeur in the West that only the "pencil of Thomas Cole or the pen of Washington Irving" could do it justice.

The wagon train set out nobly. But after only a few days on the trail, tempers began to fray, and there was grumbling by some over not being relieved on guard duty as well a "flare-up" between Alick's friend Tom Seely and a "sucker" from Illinois. Cartwright noted that there began to develop a great deal of dissatisfaction over the slow progress of the train because of the large number of wagons in it, since an accident to one delayed all.

The scenery was startling to a New Yorker, and so were the native inhabitants of the plains. The Indians were still romantic figures. One day, Cartwright and a friend took a shortcut to the next camp, and on the way met two Pottowattomie Indians. These were from the Baptist mission and quite peaceable. Cartwright inspected them closely. One young brave in particular matched Cartwright's fantasies from reading Cooper and Paulding. Cartwright compared him to an Apollo draped in a showy outfit. Cartwright added to this fellow's display of gay colors by spontaneously giving him a red silk kerchief. Continuing onto the next camp, after his first encounter with the Pottowattomies, Cartwright came upon a mass of plover and soon bagged enough for his wagon's supper. In what he called "primitive style"—meaning "Indian"—he strung them on sticks and roasted them. Very likely he began to feel a bit of an Indian himself. He continued to look for specimens of his romantic reading. Weeks further along, on the trail to the North Fork of the Platte, Cartwright had his first glimpse of a real war party of Sioux setting out against the Pawnees. Now his fantasy of the "Noble Savage" was truly fulfilled. He found the men "magnificent" and the women beautiful and was thoroughly "gratified to find some that realized the idea I had of what an Indian was in a *state of nature*." However, before the trip was over, the fantasy was thoroughly quashed by further encounters with other tribes.

The quarreling in the wagon train continued, and on the evening of April 28, Cartwright's group and five other wagons decided to leave the train and make their own way. Soon, Cartwright came down with a severe bout with dysentery, caused by eating buffalo, he believed. He rode in the wagon for nearly two weeks.

By the middle of May, less than a month on his journey, Cartwright was lonely, and his reveries give us a glimpse into his inner life. He was alone on night guard, and his sentiments drifted toward those he had left behind: "I thought of Home Sweet home! and of my Darling wife and little ones, and breathed a silent prayer to that Benificent Being who has said 'in the silent watches of the night I will be near thee,' for their protection & welfare." Just outside the light of the campfires he saw a wolf pack gathering, drawn by the remains of the supper, their eyes reflecting the fire. For him the scene was not so much dangerous as it was intensely sad and lonely. But it would be a long time before he would see his family again.

Still, he remained fascinated by the novelties of nature. He noticed bluffs of most fantastic shapes, resembling churches, castles, and even the Capitol in Washington. Others, he thought, looked like pyramids or Turkish mosques. A famous sight was "Chimney Rock." Cartwright drew a picture of it in his journal. The American West was already famous for its picturesque and monumental scenery. Cartwright noted the vast plains, cut by wild ravines and watered by numerous rivers; the gnarled and twisted cedars that lined the river banks; and the abundance of animals and birds.

Cartwright also proved to be able to write humorously. His sort of deadpan, self-deprecating style was to be developed by Mark Twain and other western humorists, of course. Indeed, Cartwright showed, as Twain was to do, an interest in western colloquial speech. We "rolled," "catched up," or "hitched up," and dozens of other western colloquialisms pepper Cartwright's account. Doubtless he was influenced by James Russell Lowell's comic colloquial figure in "Hosea Bigelow," and, indeed, a reference in the journal to the ridiculous "one-horse shay" reminds us that he also knew the poetry of Oliver Wendell Holmes. But Cartwright had a comic style of his own, too, as he displayed on May 25, when he described a mishap on the trail. Alick and two companions again took a shortcut, this time on mules, to beat the others to camp. For ten miles, things went swimmingly. But they had saddled up in haste, and in a moment all three of them lay on the prairie, their mules speeding away with their packs. At first they laughed at the comic unhorsing. Then they realized that they were stranded on the prairie without provisions or the protection of firearms. This was dangerous Indian country. Fortunately, after nearly three hours, they retraced their route back to Antoine Roubidoux's camp, and arrived to find their animals waiting for them. This was not the end of the adventure, for Robidoux, who was a famous scout, insisted that they drink a bumper of his home brewed "No. 1 brandy": "I took a bumper 'neat' but of all the drinks, that was the damndest. I can compare it to nothing but 'liquid hell fire.' I writhed and twisted in agony. My contortions of visage must have been fearful. Rushing to a bucket of water I caught up a tin cup full and tossed it down my throat, but this only appeared to aggravate it. I could feel my stomach hiss as the water came in contact with the fiery fluid. God what a ten minutes of agony I endured after that bumper of No. 1." When he finally returned to camp and related his adventures in his deadpan manner, he was "heartily laughed at."

By this time, Cartwright and his party were nearing Fort Laramie, one of the many posts of the American Fur Co. & P. Chouteau. Under the direction of Pierre Chouteau Jr., by 1849 the American Fur Company virtually monopolized the American fur trade. Originally controlled by John Jacob Astor, the American Fur Company at Fort Laramie had been styled Pratte, Chouteau & Company until 1846 and then evolved into American Fur Co. & P. Chouteau. Cartwright found a miserable set of occupants there.

From this point on, Cartwright proceeded farther west than Parkman had. The hardest part of the trail lay ahead, and Cartwright and his companions were now sufficiently experienced to know that they had brought too much unnecessary equipment. At Fort Laramie, they lightened the load in their wagon by about five hundred pounds. They still had a thousand miles to go, and they pushed on into the Black Hills. Here they encountered a party of twenty Crow Indians. It was probably this same group that later that night raided a wagon train camped nearby, rousing Cartwright from his sleep with their whoops and the report of flintlocks.

During the 1840s, because of William Bartram's influence, American travel writing of a scientific sort became vivid and acquired a statistical and scientific bent. Cartwright had shown in his creation of baseball that part of his imagination was scientific or experimental. In his journal for June 2, as they approached the Rocky Mountains, he paused to make some statistical notes and to give a summary of all he had seen. These included 20,000 buffalo, "millions" of plover, "plenty" of wolves, "thousands" of rattlesnakes, and encounters with several Indian tribes, including the Shawnee, Caw, Kansas, Sioux, Delaware, and Crow.

During his cross-country trip, Cartwright continued to play baseball, of course. By his own word, he played baseball in St. Louis and taught baseball to the men at the Boundary Line Camp. We know that with him he brought one of the balls used by the Knickerbockers, along with his rulebook and by-laws. A bat could easily be fashioned from a length of rail or a branch. Much later in life he told friends that he taught people to play baseball at nearly every stop on his journey across the plains and that it was comical to see mountain men and Indians playing the game. He expanded on this account on another occasion, indicating that he introduced the game to enthusiastic saloon-keepers and miners in California, to Indians and white settlers along the way, and at nearly every frontier town and army post that his wagon train visited. The experienced New York ballplayers who accompanied Cartwright laughed "as they watched the converts to the game attempt to imitate their own grace and skill with the bat and the ball, such as catching the ball with the hands cupped and allowing the hands to 'give' with the catch." From Cartwright's subsequent letters to former Knickerbocker teammates we can conclude that on the trail, whenever they rested and had enough people to form two baseball teams, they played ball. Peterson speculates that one such prairie baseball contest was interrupted by an Indian attack. In any event, here was the first national, cross-country baseball tour.

The overland journey left little time for sport, however. It was long, back-breaking, tedious, wearing, and full of uncertainty. It is worth putting his trip on a current map. In the first part of his journey, Cartwright passed from New York to Philadelphia, on to Pittsburgh, and then through Ohio, Indiana, and Illinois to St. Louis. He then crossed the state of Missouri to Independence. From there he traveled northerly and after much argument and tedious delays attributable to the large wagon train, he and a few friends left Russell's party at the Big Blue River just west of present-day Lincoln, Nebraska, and went forward with a handful of wagons. They followed the Platte River through Nebraska and paused at Fort Laramie, Wyoming, for rest and resupply. Their route on the Oregon Trail led them along the Sweetwater River to South Pass, Wyoming, at the Continental Divide. Once through South Pass, they rolled through Soda Springs and American Falls, Idaho, along the California Trail, then cut south through present day Elko and Winnemucca, Nevada. From here they made their way down along the Carson River into California, passing just south of Lake Tahoe, and at last arriving at Grass Valley and Fort Sutter, near Sacramento. Their long journey ended here, on the Fourth of July, 1849. Alick was free from traveling at last.

VISIONS AND REVISIONS

O f course, as it turned out, Cartwright's travels were far from over.

In Grass Valley, Cartwright made a brief investigation of his prospects of success as a miner. They were not good. The best places had already been claimed. Few new miners were making strikes, and life in the mines was woeful. Everything was in short supply, and the food and tools that were available were also astonishingly expensive. The miners themselves were in pitiable condition. "Captain Seely and I turned our attention to mining," Cartwright wrote "but after looking over the field we wisely decided that other openings offered greater inducements to men of our class." Gold fever had driven him thousands of miles across the country, but the sight of the mines and miners broke the spell in a matter of a few days. Cartwright looked around but never did a day's work in a mine.

He did the next best thing. After a little more than a month around Fort Sutter and Sacramento, he hopped on a steamboat down the Sacramento River and proceeded to San Francisco, where he arrived on August 10, 1849. He knew that Alfred had gotten there on the fifth, but what Alick couldn't know was that during the last stages of the voyage and in San Francisco, Alfred had already fallen in with two groups of investors. One group had been fellow passengers on the *Pacifico* and included the San Franciscan Mark Hopkins. The other group was from Honolulu. Both had come to San Francisco intent on sharing in the golden wealth through buying mines rather than working them. Apparently, Alfred had followed their lead, and by the time Alick arrived he had made a contact with a J. Ross Browne, who had a mine for sale. At that time Browne was a speculator in land and gold mining as well as a U.S. government agent. (Later, he would become a popular writer on western topics and a close friend of Mark Twain.) Browne was convincing concerning the prospects of his mine, and Alfred and Alick plunged ahead and bought it, perhaps in company with some of the Hawaiian or Californian investors. In 1892, shortly before Alick's death, a writer for a San Francisco paper reported an interview he had had with Alick, during which Cartwright said: "I met my younger brother Alfred [de] Forest Cartwright who had preceeded me to California by way of Cape Horn. My first business venture was the purchasing with my brother of the interest of J. Ross Browne in a mining enterprise which was being inaugurated by the party that came to San Francisco in the ship *Pacifico*."

For his part, in a letter to his wife, Rebecca, Alfred gave an account of his first meeting in San Francisco with Alick:

> Alick arrived here on the 10 instant [August 10, 1849] in good health after a long and trying journey. They lost some of their mules and broke their waggons, and were obliged to abandon most of their truck, so that Alick says they "had left what they had upon their backs, and a cup and a spoon apiece." Now where do you think he has gone to? Why, to the Sandwich Islands. He left on the 15th with a friend whom he met here and who is going into business at those islands, through whose representations he was induced to think that he could do better than by remaining here. He will probably make arrangements there to come back here with a load of fruit and vegetables, which would prove a very profitable speculation.

It was a brilliant solution—evidently better than mining and, as it turned out, definitely much better than buying a mine, since for all of Ross Browne's persuasive representations, the mine failed to "pan out" and was a total loss. However, according to one account, Alick wasted no time in introducing "baseball games between diggings." But if the miners needed anything, it was not baseball, more fantasies, more mud, or more tears, it was more food. No vegetables or fruit were grown in the vicinity of the mines. Everything had to be brought in. The surrounding areas were already hard pressed to provide an adequate supply of foodstuffs for the prospectors who were there, much less for those who were arriving daily in droves. According to Kuykendall, some sweet potatoes had been exported to the mines from Hawaii early in 1849, but the Maui potato "boom" truly exploded in the fall of 1849. Cartwright was to be in on the ground floor. According to a Maui correspondent writing to the *Polynesian*, "the call for potatoes is loud and pressing, as some vessels bound for

California have taken as many as a thousand barrels each. The price is high. . . . [Planters and merchants] will reap a rich harvest. They often repeat the saying of a foreigner, who after visiting the mines of California, came back to Maui quite satisfied, and said to his neighbor at Waikapu, . . . 'There is gold [in Maui] without the fatigue and sickness of the mining country.'" Reports came from even as far away as Hawaii that many stores in California had been stripped clean of goods to supply the miners.

The legend is probably true that during his time near the mines and in San Francisco, Alick introduced the Cartwright version of baseball, and that in this city baseball "developed into a wild sport. Professional gamblers who infested the Pacific Coast town in the early days bet heavily on the games, . . . and the 'spectators' were in the habit of shooting off revolvers when a fielder was about to catch the ball." Baseball and Cartwright arrived with a bang in the West.

Though Alick had several friends in San Francisco, he was ambivalent about staying there and soon was outward bound again. But while he remained in California, he played baseball. Cartwright had initiated games among the gold miners. It should not be surprising then, that upon arriving in San Francisco he would also have started the game up there as well. Peterson pictures him as a kind of Johnny Baseballseed, sowing the game wherever he stopped as he traveled across the country. He certainly did not do that.

But he did play a part in the development of baseball on the West Coast. Alfred DeWitt, who lived with his parents in the very house where Eliza went to give birth to the Cartwright's first son, was already in San Francisco before Alick arrived. Alick's brother Alfred also preceded him to San Francisco. Frank Turk, who played in the Knickerbockers' third recorded game, arrived in San Francisco about five weeks before Alick did. William H. Tucker arrived around the same time as Alick. Alick listed him in his journal as doing business at "271 Montgomery St. upstairs," suggesting that he had visited him there. Yet another Knickerbocker player, William R. Wheaton, disembarked in San Francisco on August 30, 1849. Alick returned to San Francisco three times in 1850 and 1851. By then other teammates of Alick's had arrived in San Francisco, including Edward A. Ebbetts and Walter Avery. Cartwright wrote at the end of his journal that Avery was to be contacted through Alfred DeWitt. Charles Case, a New York player who was not a Knickerbocker but a member of the New York Nine, arrived in San Francisco about four months before Alick.

By January 4, 1851, then, there were a sufficient number of former Knickerbockers and New York or Brooklyn players that the San Francisco "Knickerbockers Association" was founded, by-laws were set forth, a finance committee established, officers elected, and a constitution was drafted. On January 23, a resolution was drawn up, declaring that "none but those who were to the 'manor born' [i.e. gentlemen] could be considered a real genuine Knicker-bocker." The New York spirit had traveled west.

Alick had brought a Knickerbocker ball to the West, and there is every rea-son to suppose that if he had initiated games among the miners, he would have played baseball in San Francisco as well, especially when he was greeted by his former teammates and other transplanted New Yorkers who were familiar with the Cartwright version of the game. Obviously, he was in touch with the Knickerbockers in San Francisco, and it seems likely that in person or by cor-respondence he played some part in the formation of the new Knickerbocker Association. We know that by February 1851 the Knickerbockers were playing baseball in an organized form in San Francisco's Portsmouth Plaza. We even have a daguerreotype photo of a baseball game in progress in Portsmouth Plaza, dating from January 1851. But some of the earliest spontaneous games were likely to have occurred when the émigré New Yorkers, including Alick and Alfred, joined together in 1850.

Several later accounts of Cartwright's ventures have suggested that in leav-ing San Francisco for Honolulu he intended to return to New York by way of China. Such an explanation of Cartwright's journey to the Sandwich Islands can scarcely be credited, for had he intended to return to New York to join his wife and family, a trip by way of China would have involved another long and arduous journey past India and around the tip of Africa. Besides, the *Pacifico*, on which he sailed, did not travel the China route. Moreover, a decision to re-turn to New York so soon after his arrival in San Francisco following a very long journey across the continent seems highly implausible as well as uncharacter-istic of the cautious and orderly temperament that Cartwright was to exhibit all during his life. A second legend, often given in later sketches of Cartwright, is that he became ill with dysentery and was advised by a friend in San Fran-cisco, Charles Robinson, to go to the Pacific islands for his health. This, too, seems highly improbable, though it is true, as his journal shows, that he did have continuing bouts of dysentery, and he may indeed have been incidentally advised to go to Honolulu where his health might improve. (Unfortunately, he continued to experience intestinal discomforts for the remainder of his life.) Yet another story was that he intended to go to China, but he had a bout of dys-entery on the ship to Hawaii and "had to be put ashore in Honolulu." Perhaps the best and most general reason for Cartwright's decision to continue on to

Hawaii was given in a Hawaiian newspaper clipping: "Mining, however, though it was at its height when he was in California, did not have the lure for him that it had for others. Honolulu was very new in those days, and he was looking for something newer than the mainland offered[,] so he came."

Alfred's letter gives the soundest specific reasons for Cartwright's departure from San Francisco. Clearly, Alick seized upon the opportunity to go to Honolulu to engage in business with his and Alfred's new acquaintances, who had come to California from Hawaii to invest in gold mining. As Alfred surmised, Alick intended to bring foodstuffs back from Hawaii to the mines. Hardly had he ended his arduous cross-continent trip when he embarked for Honolulu on the *Pacifico* on August 15, 1849. He listed his profession as "merchant" in his passport, and a merchant he was determined to be. The delegation of investors from Honolulu booked passage on the *Pacifico*, too, the same ship on which Alfred had rounded the horn. On August 24, 1849, Alick landed in Honolulu, where a new adventure commenced. Or perhaps his adventures simply continued, for many more were to follow.

PARADISE FOUND

Before the *Pacifico* sailed into the port of Honolulu, Alick had learned that A. B. Howe, who had been a friend of Alick's father in New York, was doing business in Hawaii. Upon docking, Cartwright located Howe. It was a lucky meeting, since here, without delay, was a job. Honolulu then was pretty much still a village of grass huts with a scattering of foreigners' houses and a tangle of warehouses and crude business buildings. Howe owned a flourishing ship-chandlery business, provisioning merchantmen with necessary supplies. He needed a bookkeeper. Alick's training at Union Bank and his conduct of his own business had made him an excellent accountant, a talent he had also applied to keeping precise records of baseball games. Even more important and urgent, Howe had already made plans to be absent from Honolulu in California for an extended period of time, and he decided that Cartwright was a man he could trust to take care of his business in his absence. Very likely at this time Alick confided to Howe his idea of shipping foodstuffs to the coast and selling them to the miners. In short order, Howe offered Alick a job. This offer, a writer for the *Commercial Record* asserts, "Cartwright gladly accepted." Evidently his conduct of business met Howe's expectations. And "after Howe's return from 'the Coast,' [Howe]... charted the brig *Pacifico*[,] which he loaded with sweet potatoes, and induced Mr. Cartwright to go to California as supercargo." This journalist added the remark that "Mr. Cartwright... planned to remit to Mr. Howe the proceeds of the venture, and remain in America. He had no intention of returning to Honolulu." But it turned out otherwise.

Howe was to prove a good model for the way in which a newcomer to Hawaii could build toward success. He supplied ships, he purchased land that would be developed into a sugar plantation, he got an authorization to "sell at public auction licenses to sell spirituous liquors at retail," and so on. The plain fact was that there were plenty of commercial opportunities in 1840s and 1850s Hawaii, but no one of them was yet secure enough for a cautious businessman to specialize in: success came from following multiple opportunities. Cartwright would learn this lesson well—to be nimble in a new country.

Clearly, Cartwright was a bit at loose ends, uncertain where to settle. Alfred had remained in San Francisco to explore opportunities there. The brothers had made the journey to the West Coast without their wives, and now that they had jointly decided not to commit themselves to work in the gold fields, a heavy responsibility lay on them to choose new careers and establish themselves in them. The longer they delayed, the greater would be the length of time before they could send for their wives and children. Alick set out to be an entrepreneur, a merchant. Doubtless, he had additional reasons for thinking about returning to California. Aside from hoping for a share of the profit from the potato shipment, Alick seized the chance to return to San Francisco to consult with his brother and to discover what headway Alfred had made. His letters in later years suggest that on balance at this time he was inclined to settle in San Francisco and eventually go in business with Alfred. But where he would finally live was still undetermined.

Potatoes, the food the miners most needed, was just what Hawaii produced, and Alick and Howe's venture in potatoes was a great success. Not only sweet potatoes but "Irish potatoes" filled the hold of the ship. Both varieties of tuber grew plentifully on the cool slopes of the Haleekala volcano in Maui, where by the late 1820s Irish and sweet potato cultivation had become of great importance. By 1847, 20,000 barrels of Irish potatoes were grown there. That island's Kula area was so well adapted to them that it was already known as "the potato district." When the profits from his cargo exceeded all expectations, Cartwright's mind tilted away from San Francisco. The Sandwich Islands might prove to be the true goldmine in the West. For his part, Alfred had not settled upon anything firm in San Francisco. The result was predictable. Honolulu and Lahaina would become Alick's homes. And so Alick was a passenger on the *Pacifico* when it made the return trip to Hawaii. True, he expected to return to San Francisco again, but it would be with another ship's hold full of food to sell to the miners or the distributors who served the gold fields. Hawaii was to be his base.

THE LAST GASP OF THE GREAT SAILING SHIPS

By May of 1850 Alick was on the wing again with another cargo of potatoes and, this time, with some tropical fruits in addition. Again, the voyage was a success. He was no longer thinking of remaining on the mainland. Before three weeks had passed he had disposed of his entire cargo. By the second week of June he was ready to start back to Honolulu. Many ships were leaving daily, but he was induced to wait for the June 16 departure of the *Samuel Russell*. The reasons this vessel strongly appealed to him are clear. Having been in Pacific waters previously, the ship had recently sailed from New York around Cape Horn. In the East, it had established a reputation as a fast sailing ship, and for a descendant of seagoing ancestors, as Alick was, there was an air of adventure in this sailing, since many people speculated that the *Russell* would set a record for the most rapid passage from San Francisco to the Sandwich Islands. The numerous members of the Nantucket branch of Alick's family had lived their lives and made their careers in sailing ships. His own father had been a ship captain. And Alick took pride in the continuing supremacy of the traditionally rigged vessels. In the late 1840s and 1850s, the question of whether or when the new oceanic steamships would surpass the speed of sailing ships was much discussed. The *Russell* had moved faster than the steamships in the East. Excitedly, Cartwright booked passage. He bought a new notebook to record the daily progress and followed the same procedure that he had adopted in keeping baseball records and in his journal of his journey across the country. He would first make notes and then use them to write up a more fully composed and smooth account afterward. He now began to see that the journey across the country had not ended on the coast but was merely the initial phase of the long journey that would end only in Honolulu. He was ready to be associated with a new speed record and to be its chronicler.

Cartwright was one of the many Americans in the 1850s who began to be interested in speed—speed to populate the continent, speed to turn the Horn or cross the Pacific, speed to establish commerce on American terms. Americans were in a hurry. Speed was to remain an American preoccupation for a long time. Compared to cricket, baseball, too, was a speedy game and a game of speed.

So Cartwright walked up the gangplank of the *Samuel Russell*, found his cabin, opened his record book, and began his sequel to his overland journey. In this new journal of his voyage, he noted that he had "engaged passage" on June 15 on the *Russell*, "which has the reputation of being the fastest clipper ship in the world." He wrote down a title parallel to that of his overland journey: "Journal of a Voyage from San Francisco to Sandwich Islands." Charles P. Low, he recorded, was part owner and the master of the *Russell*. He listed the five other passengers who accompanied him. He was meticulous in his details, giving the dimensions of the *Russell*: length (180 feet), breadth (35 feet, 4 inches), depth of hold (22 feet), and tonnage (971 tons).

On June 16, with a fresh morning wind blowing, they sailed out of San Francisco Bay. Cartwright's hopes for a new record were flying faster than the ship. By the next morning the ship had sailed 300 miles. With considerable excitement, Cartwright wrote down the remarkable records for speed previously made by the *Russell*, and he ventured to predict that if the wind held up it would beat any of the ocean steamers. The first mate encouraged Cartwright with the statistic that the ship could move at fourteen knots. "She cuts through the water like a North River streamer, limber and very sharp and she leaves a cleaner wake than any ship I have ever seen," he wrote.

A fine beginning. But on the evening of June 18 the wind died, and the *Russell* averaged only five knots through the night. Would they resume a vigorous speed? Would the winds return? They didn't, and the voyagers lost the record they confidently expected. Finally, the ship lagged into Honolulu harbor on July 1, 1850.

Cartwright was writing at the tipping point of maritime history, and his heart clearly was with the sailing ships whose day was almost done. On the *Russell*, he himself was living out the last days of the sailing ship's preeminence.

MISSIONARY BASEBALL

By the spring of 1850 Cartwright had spent extended periods on the island of Maui securing contracts for the potatoes and other vegetables that grew on the slopes there. Other business possibilities existed on the island as Hawaii was fast becoming a mercantile center. Lahaina was heavily invested in the whaling industry that still flourished in the 1830s and 1840s. The rapidly increasing populations of California and Oregon powerfully stimulated trade, especially after the discovery of gold. When Cartwright relocated to Maui in 1850, the island was bustling with enterprising merchants and opportunities for trade. In 1850 Cartwright was shuttling back and forth between Maui and Honolulu, where he worked for Howe, and he had not given up his own personal food export activities. In 1851, he made a third trip to San Francisco with a boatload of vegetables and fruits. No fantasies of record speeds survived his disappointment in the *Samuel Russell*, and he traveled to San Francisco on the bark *Yankee*, later returning to Honolulu on the *Isabella*, both reliable, workaday ships. Little could Cartwright know as he left San Francisco in 1851 that this would be the last time that he would see the mainland. For the next forty-one years he would live out his life in Hawaii.

Baseball preceded Cartwright to Hawaii, and from the most unexpected quarter: the activities of Christian missionaries in the Sandwich Islands. In 1819, the missionary impulse was felt strongly at Yale University and Cornwall, Connecticut, where plans to create a foreign mission school were begun. A meeting was held at the Park Street Church in Boston. There a band of Congregationalist missionaries was formed and prepared to go to the Sandwich Islands to bring Christianity to the natives. Two ministers, Hiram Bingham and Asa Thurston, two school teachers, a printer, a physician, a farmer, and their wives, together with the three young native Hawaiians who had come to Boston to study, formed the first company of missionaries to the islands. The first contingent left Boston on the *Thaddeus* on October 23, 1819. Over the next decades, missionaries were typically sent out in such "companies."

This first mission to the Sandwich or Hawaiian islands was organized by the American Board of Commissionaries for Foreign Missions. This was an interdenominational Christian organization, but its members were predominantly Presbyterian and Congregational. Kuykendall writes that the missionary movement to Hawaii "was the outgrowth of two forces: the evangelical revival," or the Second Great Awakening in the United States in the late eighteenth century, along with "the operations of the New England traders in the Pacific Ocean." Both combined to call attention to the presence in Hawaii of a population that had already shown a disposition to learn Christian teachings.

Certainly, the missionaries were primarily interested in the salvation of souls, but they were also bent on the enlightenment of minds and "had a clear conception of their role as a civilizing agency." In addition to an awareness of Christ and an acquaintance with Scripture, they also wanted to introduce "the arts and institutions and usages of civilized life and society" to the Hawaiians. This meant simply that they were intent on Americanizing the islands. The missionaries who traveled to Hawaii brought American values with them. By 1840, they could be found in all parts of the Hawaiian kingdom, and since they devoted themselves chiefly to the education and Christian instruction of children, their influence became more and more pervasive over the years. They quickly founded schools for the education of native Hawaiians, such as the Lahainaluna Seminary in 1831, the Hilo Boarding School in 1836, and the Chief's Children's School in 1839, but they established no schools for the children of missionaries.

One of the institutions of American civilization was clearly sports, and ball games were predominant among these. The missionaries would not tolerate native Hawaiian games that involved gambling—*pahee* or *panhenehene*—and New England games such as marbles, chess, or cards were also disallowed because they, too, involved gambling. Nor did they allow such entertainments as dancing. Even as they banned all these among their young charges, they wisely knew that the young needed games to play, and so they substituted acceptable American games for indigenous ones. Base-ball was the inevitable game of choice for the missionaries to encourage among the natives. The Hawaiians readily took to baseball, for they had had their own ball games. The one most closely paralleling baseball was called *kinipopo*. It was played with bats made of *hau* (hibiscus) trees, and employed a round ball made of cloth. "Bases" were even marked in *kinipopo* by stuffed cloth bags. Baseball and Christ came to Hawaii at the same moment.

The missionaries' concern for the education and moral well-being of their own children provided a second impetus for the establishment of baseball. It was evident early on that the missionary children who grew up in Hawaii and among Hawaiians would not necessarily become "Americans," a national value highly cherished by all Americans in the early nineteenth century. Individual missionary parents were not willing to have their children adopt Hawaiian customs, attitudes, and habits. "Many of [our children] . . . have no associates unless we permit them to associate with the heathen, which indeed we cannot always prevent," the minutes of the Presidential Committee of the Mission Family lamented. They needed to find a way to keep their children "American" even as they grew up abroad. Baseball was one such way.

The most extreme measure to keep the missionary children "Americanized" involved sending them back to the mainland. As early as the 1820s, it seemed necessary to missionary parents to send young children to America for their education. This, however, proved to be unworkable. Besides the difficult six-month sea journey back to New England that children had to take alone, the practice made for a virtually permanent separation between parents and children and an immense burden of grief on both sides. For some families, this meant that parents would never see their children again, for children raised in the United States often lacked the Christianizing fervor of their parents and usually remained in America. "It was a great trial . . . to part with them," one missionary wife wrote her father. After she saw her children depart the islands, she returned home to a lonely house: "When husband returned we mingled our tears together, gathered our remaining little ones around us, kneeled down and committed our dear absent ones to the kind Shepherd of Israel." Some better solution than separation at the tender age of six or seven had to be reached, and an obvious solution was at hand. The Honolulu school at Punahou was founded in May 1841, in a small building adjacent to Kanwiaiahao Church, near Hiram Bingham's old house. The school was originally called Oahu College, but soon became Punahou ("none so beloved"). In 1839 Queen Kaahumanu gave Mr. and Mrs. Hiram Bingham land at Punahou for the use of the mission. The school there actually opened on July 11, 1842. And, of course, on Saturdays, and when the young students had recess, they played ball games. Indeed, it appears that the missionaries insisted that "base-ball" be a part of the their children's day, since it was thought to be a major element in the process of Americanization. Mark Twain's later remark that "Baseball is the very symbol, the outward and visible expression of the drive and push and rush and struggle of the raging, tearing, booming [American] nineteenth century" was echoed by most Americans. Even missionary fathers and mothers agreed and urged their children to remain Americans while in foreign parts by playing the national game. Besides, baseball was ritualistic and orderly, unlike many other games. The missionaries liked that.

The Punahou school, one historian has asserted, became "the center for the teaching and playing of baseball." Frank Ardolino writes that the "missionaries established Punahou to . . . foster the creation of a new society in Hawaii dedicated to Protestantism and the American values of capitalism, competition, and progressivism. Their children learned these values and in the process developed baseball as a major expression" of the core of Americanism. The missionaries' church had its own rituals, but the rules of baseball, soon to be established by Alexander Cartwright on the mainland, became the central codes and rituals of their quest for nationality.

C. P. Goto claims that Captain James H. Black, the Boston printer who came to Hawaii with Hiram Bingham's company and had a printing shop at the corner of Liliha and Vineyard, introduced American baseball—doubtless rounders—to Hawaii. Black, Goto says, brought baseball equipment "from Boston around Cape Horn, and he taught the Hawaiian youngsters how to hit and catch." One early game of ball played there resembled cricket. "The boys," Cisco writes, "used two batters at a time and called their game 'aipuni.'" At a very early date, in the 1820s, Black taught the rules and the practice of New England base-ball. As a result, even before Punahou was founded, Goto writes, "baseball was established as a popular pastime in the islands, for both native Hawaiians and the Americans who emigrated there."

Precisely when base-ball made its first appearance in Hawaii is a matter of interpretation. The indigenous game itself was not likely to qualify as baseball. What game was meant in the *Polynesian* when, in 1840, a writer in that journal referred to the "good old bat-and-ball" game—as if some "old" form of baseball had been played in Hawaii for a very long time? Frank Boardman was more specific when, in 1910, he asserted that at least as far as his own memory, which carried back to 1842, "baseball had been played . . . under the name of *rounders*, one-old-cat, two-old-cat, and townball."

Curtis J. Lyons was more specific as to the place where baseball first flourished. In 1901, he asserted that the boys at Punahou school were the first to play baseball in the Islands after it had been introduced in the early 1840s by a Boston clergyman. Certainly, baseball was avidly played at the Punahou school, where children of the missionaries and other mainland youth were educated.

S. F. Furukawa claims that in its modern form, "Cartwright introduced baseball to the Islanders." Albert Brown Lyons remembered seeing baseball at Punahou soon after his arrival in 1857. In 1860 the *Polynesian* reported that "quite an interesting game of ball came off yesterday afternoon on the Esplanade between the Punahou boys and the Town boys." The first game in which statistics were officially recorded was played in 1866 on a field that later became the site of the Central Union Church. At that game, Cisco writes:

The Natives beat the Foreigners 2-1. Another game from that era was held in August of 1867 on the lot makai (seaward) of the Punahou campus. The Pacifics downed the Pioneers 11-9. A Punahou girls' team was formed in 1874. Punahou's boys played against the Atkinson School in 1878 and by 1888 played regular competition against such teams as the Honolulus, Vandalias, Stars, and Hawaiis.

"Cartwright," Cisco says flatly, "helped to popularize the sport." Perhaps it is best simply to say that quite soon baseball as Cartwright had codified it was first identified with the Punahou school. We know that Cartwright sent his children to Punahou and that he was deeply involved in both the academic and the sports activities there. An amusing letter of November 1859 shows that Alick was helping his children with their homework and finding the arithmetic texts used in the school "exceedingly" puzzling. The fault seems to have been in the textbook, for Cartwright was an excellent accountant and besides, a Dr. Hildebrand and Reverend Samuel C. Damon also found the book, Thompson's *Arithmetic*, confusing. If he was so involved that he was reading the children's arithmetic books, he was certainly also following and supporting baseball there. The first historian of baseball in Hawaii writes that when Cartwright arrived in Honolulu he "taught the youngsters the new game behind the old court house," which building later became a storehouse for the American Factors company.

Baseball flourished at Punahou. The oldest pupil at the school, Orramel Gulick, age eleven, wrote in a letter that the boys (and most of the girls) were "passionately fond of open-air sports, such as . . . [the Hawaiian ball game] *a-puni* . . . [and] wicket. . . . Bat and ball was the standard game. . . . In the early forties Hon. Charles R. Bishop [a trustee] used to come up on Saturdays expressly to have a game with enthusiastic youngsters at the school." Orramel's brother William added a note about the master of Punahou, Reverend Daniel Dole. He would "throw a ball into the air, and as it fell, with a swing of his whole body, would hit it with the report of a pistol, sending it straight up into the air almost out of sight." Pertinently, the ball that Dole batted almost out of sight had to be a dense one by the mid-1840s, suggesting that in Hawaii the game may have no longer involved plugging a runner. Indeed, we know, in further confirmation of this supposition, that the players scattered sandbags upon the grass to mark bases. Instructed by the school administration and teachers, the boys made their own bats. James and Levi Chamberlain marched into the Manoa valley and cut bats from *kukui* and *hau* branches. They peeled off the bark and laid the branches in the sun to dry.

Of course, Black and the missionaries were probably teaching the Hawaiian and Yankee children the New England game of rounders that they had played in their own youth. With the arrival of New Yorkers, the game shifted toward New York's town-ball game. Either way, baseball at Punahou had become, even in the youngsters, the central ritual of American leisure and social contact. One of the earliest graduates of Punahou, Albert Brown Lyons, later a valedictorian at Williams College, remembered the school for "experiences of diversified activities not belonging to the curriculum of study." Primary was "baseball (in primitive form) and wicket," that is, "cricket."

The native Hawaiian students were taught American baseball along with American Christianity. The missionary children at Punahou were introduced to two powerful reasons to make baseball flourish in Hawaii. They had balls, bats, experienced adult rounders and town-ball players, meadows, and bases. What seems to be lacking was the concept of a diamond-shaped field and a game with uniform and scientific rules. Baseball in Hawaii was waiting for the arrival of Alexander Joy Cartwright Jr.

STARTING ALL OVER AGAIN

It's Gonna be Rough—but We're Gonna Make It

W hen Cartwright first stepped off the *Pacifico* in 1849 he walked into a town in which nearly everything was still to be made. Honolulu was a city of low, small, wooden buildings huddled around the docks. Its commerce remained vastly underdeveloped. Business opportunities were everywhere, but the economic structures required for their realization were still absent. Public services were barely organized. A school system and institutions for public protection—police and fire departments, for instance—were at best rudimentary and at worst entirely absent. Cultural institutions, such as the arts, public charities, and organizations for personal improvement, social connection, or commercial progress were virtually nonexistent, hoped-for but unrealized. To be sure, churches were well established, and religious organizations for spiritual and educational outreach were beginning to be active. The children of the original missionaries were entering society and would eventually dominate commercial life. But still it may fairly be said that Honolulu was a great vacuum into which new citizens could rush and prosper. Cartwright walked into a world of possibility. Such a world, of course, was also chancy. The very lack of development and secure, well-established foundations for activity ensured that there would be as great a likelihood of failure as of success.

Cartwright's association with Aaron B. Howe seemed promising. After all, Howe was an experienced businessman and had proved himself capable of establishing and running a successful ship chandlery business. And he evidently trusted Cartwright. Together, Howe and Cartwright borrowed $1,000 from William E. Gill on November 21, 1851, to develop joint businesses. Then Howe died unexpectedly in the following year. In a stable society with long-established firms, individuals could pass in and out while a business continued. But in

Hawaii, all businesses were still so new that their continuance depended heavily on the people who founded them. So when Howe died, the business died with him, being simply absorbed by other ship chandlers such as Swan and Clifford. Cartwright was out of a job just as this one had seemed so secure.

Fortunately, he had accumulated a small supply of capital through the profits accruing from his sales of foodstuffs to the mainland, especially intended for the minefields where the ground "grew" only gold, if anything at all. Nearly all of the potatoes were grown on the rich volcanic slopes of Maui. And because of this, Cartwright had become acquainted with several of the leading businessmen in Lahaina.

Richard H. Bowlin was one of these. At loose ends, Cartwright listened to a business proposition from Bowlin in 1851. The records and account books kept by Bowlin show that his varied businesses were undercapitalized and also that Bowlin himself, though widely respected as a person, lacked the accounting and managerial skills necessary for successful entrepreneurship. By contrast, Cartwright had a small stock of cash and was looking for a place to invest it, and his skills as an accountant and manager had been tested and proven both in New York and in association with Howe. Finally, Cartwright's ventures in food supply and his rapidly acquired knowledge of the agricultural production of Maui were directly relevant to his new business, a large part of which involved provisioning and resupplying ships with comestibles. Cartwright was in on the ground floor in this, since Maui's agricultural production had begun to expand noticeably only since 1848.

Bowlin knew a good man when he saw one. He proposed that Cartwright join him in partnership and invest his potato profits in a new firm: Bowlin and Cartwright. Everything about this business promised success. First of all, it was diversified. Its flagship was a hotel, designed and furnished to attract the whalers who regularly made a stop in Lahaina. It had a bowling alley and a billiard room for their entertainment and well-furnished hotel rooms for their periodic stays on land. Of course, other businessmen who visited Lahaina would also be keen to stay at the very place where whalers congregated. On the ground floor of the hotel was a general merchandise store, relying heavily on the whalers but also supplying the growing number of residents in Lahaina, the undisputed capital of Maui. Shifting their commercial ventures away from Lahaina, Cartwright and Bowlin also opened up two stores that sold staples and supplies to the residents and the men who docked in the ports of Kalului and Kula and the surrounding areas. Alick set out to put the books in order, strengthen the economic base of the stores, and develop the business.

Cartwright had every reason to look confidently upon the prospects for the firm of Bowlin and Cartwright. Beside the diversity of the enterprise, Lahaina was a well established whaling port, the best one within a radius of two thousand miles. Certainly, he and Bowlin were sufficiently confident in the success of their business that on March 10, 1851, they applied to the Hawaii government for a lease on lots 7 and 8, amounting to about an acre, in the port of Kalului. They asked for a fifty-year lease at an annual rental of $100. This plan to acquire new property was clearly meant to augment their store in Kalului and allow them to supply whalers directly from the docks. Kahului was destined to become the island's second port. The Interior Department considered the application favorably and recommended it to King Kamehameha III, who approved it without modification.

Lahaina remained the main port on Maui, but now the new firm had a presence in the other two ports at which whalers and traders might stop. Ever since the discovery in 1819 of the sperm whale grounds off the coast of Japan, Maui had been the main stop for whalers in Pacific waters. But Pacific whaling got a spectacular boost in 1846, just three years before Cartwright's arrival, when new grounds were located along the Ohnotsk and Bering Straits and in the Arctic Ocean. The prospects for continued expansion seemed unlimited. And true enough, whaling stops in Lahaina reached higher and higher in 1846, 1853, and 1859, with more than 500 ships docking in Lahaina, Kahului, and Honolulu in each of those years.

Richard Bowlin, too, gave every appearance of being a sound partner to Alick. A lawyer by profession, he had grown up in Missouri then immigrated to California. Finally, he had come to the islands for his health. But in the flux of 1850s Hawaiian society, when new opportunities seemed to come along daily, Bowlin appeared to have a flighty character. During the early months of their partnership, as Alick was settling in, the attorney Bowlin was offered the position of police magistrate of Honolulu, in place of C. G. Hopkins, who had resigned. He accepted the offer and was commissioned on April 27, 1851, and from this date began to try to move back and forth between Honolulu and Lahaina to keep both jobs going. This juggling act was never to be workable. By all reports, Bowlin made an excellent police magistrate, but now Cartwright was left to do his own juggling, keeping the stores and hotel and agricultural supplies and cash flow all in good shape. The task would have taken the efforts of two men.

For one it was all but impossible, and the business soon began to show signs of decline. The Bowlin and Cartwright "Cash Journal" account books, which begin on February 1, 1850, and carry on with some gaps until October 1, 1851, show that the firm was constantly struggling to raise cash, stock the stores, and keep the hotel and its amenities in good operating condition. Even before Bowlin became an absentee partner, the two men had been compelled to seek a loan from the Treasury Department. The records of the Privy Council, whose approval was required, show that on February 21, 1850, the Council resolved that the application of Messrs. Bowlin and Cartwright of Lahaina for a loan of $1,500 mortgage in property be granted. The $1,500, however, soon evaporated in the managerial disorder of the business. Cartwright attempted to bolster the business with an infusion of capital by taking another boatload of potatoes and fruit to California, but this meant further managerial inattention. The result was that a year and a half after the loan was approved, the partners were unable to meet their obligation to the Treasury Department. The Privy Council considered the situation and agreed to postpone payment for another six months until March 1, 1852. But this was postponing the inevitable. When the note came due after six months, the loan could not be repaid. Consequently, in April 1852, the firm of Bowlin and Cartwright filed for bankruptcy. By the end of 1852, its property was auctioned, and the proceeds went to the settlement of the loan. The partnership was dissolved.

Many similar business failures had occurred in Hawaii, where speculation was rampant, and neither Bowlin nor Cartwright seems to have suffered a loss of reputation. Indeed, when Bowlin retired from his office as police magistrate he entered into business with Alick's brother Alfred de Forest Cartwright. Together, they opened general merchandise stores on Maui, in Kalului and Kalepolepo.

Despite the firm's bankruptcy, Cartwright was building a reputation in Hawaii as a thoroughly reliable man, and his affable disposition began to attract some of the leading businessmen, along with some members of the native Hawaiian royal government. With the failure of his enterprises in Maui, Cartwright moved to Honolulu to start all over again. In the basically unstable "frontier" business society of Hawaii, failure was not discreditable. "Try and try again" was the motto there.

In September 1852, Alick was hired as a bookkeeper by the firm of Richard Coady & Co., "at a very remunerative salary." Coady's firm was another ship chandlery business, and Cartwright fit right in. Not only was his salary good, but he was given assurances by Coady himself that his work could earn him a partnership in the company. But once more, Cartwright was disappointed. Apparently, Coady's pressing need for an expert bookkeeper led him to promise more than he intended or could deliver. For two years, Cartwright kept his shoulder to the wheel and saw his work meet with unqualified approval. But as the expiration of his contract drew near, he was bitter. On August 16, 1853, he wrote a despairing letter about the Coady firm to George D. Cassio, now married to Alick's favorite sister, Kate, and once Alick's teammate on the Knickerbockers. George was one of the few people to whom Alick could speak openly about his disappointments. He wrote to him that in Coady's he had been "fully wronged." He paused to reflect upon the ventures with Howe and Bowlin. With so many setbacks to his hopes, in New York, in California, and now in Honolulu, he told George, he had nearly despaired. Too often he had been a "dammed fool" to trust in men's promises. But now, he vowed, the scales had fallen from his eyes, and henceforth he would look reality in the face.

To be sure, he would never become as self-seeking as he here resolved to be. It was fundamental in Alick's personality that he would always continue to be mindful and trusting of others. Even by the end of this letter he urged George not to mention any of his disappointments to Kate for fear she would worry for him.

Cartwright's commitment to principle and a basic optimism were always a marked feature of his character. He had signed a two-year contract with Coady and he was determined to honor it. As the term of his agreement neared on March 28, 1854, he wrote to a friend who was a well known captain of a whaler out of New Bedford, Massachusetts, James Lee Edgar, that he still hoped to see the promises made to him kept. But if not, he would survive. He was no longer desperate. He immediately perked up and added that despite all, "I am sure of a comfortable subsistence for my family and may perchance have a show for something better."

In fact, he continued at R. Coady & Co. until August 1, 1856, retaining a resilient and stoic attitude and evidently making use of the networking possibilities arising from work with that firm. He called for contract arbitration over the promises of partnership made to him in writing. And when he finally separated from Coady's, he wrote to William F. Dow that the partners at Coady's had his best wishes, if they would only let him alone: "all I want is a clear field and no favor." As it happened, Coady & Co. was on a downhill slide, going out of business in late 1858, even as Alick's fortunes were by then decidedly looking up.

In fact, Alick was now poised for the beginnings of success, but it did not come out of the blue. All the time that Alick was employed at Coady's, he was busy meeting members of the Honolulu business elite, making friends, and even associating with royal members of the government. All this started in a most surprising way. Just as he got bookkeeping positions by virtue of his early work for Union Bank in New York, so now his previous membership in the Knicker-bocker firefighting company called attention to him.

Honolulu was a city of wooden buildings. Far more than New York, whose progress in erecting brick and masonry buildings was going rapidly forward, Honolulu was a conflagration waiting to happen. The downtown area near the port was already crowded with wooden wharves, store houses, and customs offices. Just behind these the business buildings, in which trade was organized and records kept, were all wooden structures. Beyond that, the residences were also wooden. Several fires had broken out in the 1840s, but so far the city had been lucky not to suffer a total conflagration.

Reason would have argued for the rapid creation of a city fire department, or at least volunteer companies. But the absence of a big disaster allowed preparations to languish. In 1847, the city gained access to—not ownership of—its first piece of fire-fighting equipment. This was a hand engine and pumper actually owned by a private Chinese firm, Sam Sing Company. Unfortunately, it was wholly inadequate beyond the possible protection of a single owner's property. As a historian of firefighting in Honolulu wrote, it was "a very diminutive arrangement, and constructed on a very rude plan, water being bailed into it by buckets." This pumper was hardly more effective than buckets of water thrown upon a blaze. The first time it was used by the city, the hose burst, and the city had to pay to replace the hose with a new one manufactured in leather. No wonder that a city ordinance was soon passed that required each citizen of Honolulu to keep two buckets always at hand for emergencies in fighting fires. Except for this provision, Honolulu had no firefighters and no fire chief.

By 1850 something had to be done. On November 6, 1850, W. C. Parke was appointed fire chief by the city council, with the mandate to organize a department, but he seems never to have made any efforts toward this goal. While the city waited, the inevitable occurred. A sudden fire destroyed a dozen homes in Honolulu. At this point King Kamehameha III forcefully stepped in and demanded that a city fire department be created without further delay. Several documents in the Hawaii State Archives tell the story of what happened at this crucial point. Three of the most influential businessmen in Honolulu, Charles R. Castle, Robert G. Davis, and Charles Brewer, approached the government with a request identical to Kamehameha's demand. Cartwright's involvement in the Knickerbocker company was known to these and other influential men, and the fact that he had been involved in fighting several big blazes in New York impressed them. They soon made a request of the Hawaiian government that Cartwright be appointed chief engineer of the fire department of the city of Honolulu. He was, they asserted, the most capable, fit, and proper person to fill the said office. With Kamehameha's support the Privy Council met and swiftly passed legislation creating "An Act to Organize the Fire Department of the City of Honolulu." The bill was accepted at once and signed by his majesty in Privy Council on December 27, 1850. It was then sent to Kekuanaoia, the governer of Oahu, who pressed it into action and appointed Cartwright chief engineer. Technically, Alick was the second fire chief appointed, but forever after he was regarded as Honolulu's first chief. On February 3, 1851, he was duly commissioned, and, as H. A. Smith remarked, "from that time forward the department flourished."

He started slowly because he was still trying to keep the Bowlin and Cartwright dream afloat. Perhaps he speculated that with the public services of the city organized around the police department (where Bowlin was preeminent) and the fire department (where he was chief) the business might get a boost. He moved ahead methodically, his experience in New York with the Knickerbocker Engine Co. no. 12, as well as his engagement in creating the rules of baseball and the by-laws for a team, having taught Cartwright exactly what he had to do first: pick up his pen. Just as the government of the United States had essentially come into existence through the writing of the Constitution and the Knickerbocker engine company and Knickerbocker baseball teams in New

York and San Francisco had also been created by books of by-laws, so now the Honolulu Fire Department came into existence by way of a constitution and written rules. Cartwright bought a notebook and sat down to write its first by-laws and constitution. As one reporter put it, Alick "brought into the department all of the customs and rules of the New York volunteers department . . . which conditions would permit."

At first, of course, there was little for Alick to do. There was no fire house, no fire equipment, no corps of fireman—only Cartwright's constitution. He let his plans mature and devised the structure of his organization as he juggled his business in Lahaina and his adventures in potatoes. Almost nine months after his appointment he was ready to send to John Young, Hawaiian minister of the interior, a brief report on his progress. Shortly before filing this report, Cartwright had worked effectively to promote a public subscription for the purpose of acquiring a new pump. He raised a sufficient amount of money, and in August 1851 he purchased a new hand engine through Brewer & Company. On September 17, 1851, he wrote to Young that insomuch as he had been importuned to form a hook and ladder company, he had now succeeded in enlisting fifty ready volunteers who were prepared to fight fires in Honolulu, along with a carriage and apparatus.

Progress was being made slowly. About a year later, Cartwright made his second big purchase for the Fire Department. On December 30, 1852, he sent J. C. Spalding a payment of $1,300 for the purchase of "one Fire Engine." By April of the next year this pumper—named Boston Engine No. 3—was already in need of repair, and it cost the city four days of work by Richard Halliday to fix it. Of course, temporary housing had to be located for the pumper, and a crude firehouse was constructed. Cartwright now had the true beginnings of a fire department. In the meantime, he and his volunteers had been busy seeing to it that Honolulu was cleared of combustibles, and no new major fires had been allowed in the city.

By 1855, Cartwright was ready to propose that a new, permanent fire house be built. The government actively supported his plan. Prince Lot—later to be King Kamehameha V—endorsed a proposal written by Cartwright to the Privy Council respecting a location for an engine house. The Privy Council referred the plan to a committee of Allen and Hopkins. In turn, their favorable report was adopted pro forma, and a new engine house was speedily approved.

Cartwright remained fire chief from December 1850 until June of 1859. Various payments of bills for repairs of fire equipment show Cartwright's continuing attentiveness to the maintenance of the department. As late as 1858 he was still attending personally to the purchase of various equipment and hoses; for instance, he paid J. H. Wood $9.75 for a leather hose in 1858.

On the occasion of his retirement he was presented with a magnificent chief's trumpet, with which he was often photographed. He had taken the job and performed his duties without calculation, but his performances as a crucial and reliable civic servant gave him access to the king, Prince Lot, the Privy Council, the minister of the interior, and Honolulu's business leaders, since all these were intensely concerned that no massive fires should devastate the city and retard its rapidly advancing but still fragile economy. Indeed, during Cartwright's watch, King Kamehameha III himself became a volunteer member of the first hook and ladder company. As H. A. Smith nicely writes, Cartwright's department "lay claim to having the only Fire Department in the world which has had kings as active members. Kamehameha III, who reigned during the '50s, took an immensely active interest in the department." Indeed, this monarch could be seen "shedding [his coat], rolling up [his] sleeves, and digging in with other red-shirted volunteers."

Cartwright retired in full glory. But his status as a guardian of the city was increased still further when his successor failed to measure up to the standard that Alick had set. As a result he was strenuously importuned to resume his former post. He agreed to this as a temporary arrangement and spent the year from July 1, 1862, to June 30, 1863, as fire chief, during which time he assisted in the search for a permanent replacement. Upon his earlier retirement he had joined Mechanic Engine Company no. 2 as a volunteer, first reporting on June 7, 1859. Now, in 1863, he returned to membership in that company and so for years to come retained a valuable association with fire fighting. To Cartwright's effective organization of the fire department was attributable the almost complete absence of major fires in the city. Small blazes were extinguished rapidly, before they could spread. Not until 1887 was there a major destructive fire in "our little city."

Cartwright's activities as fire chief were modeled upon the practices in New York. There, the fire companies had developed into powerful civic and political institutions and also promoted sporting events, picnics, dances, and other social occasions. He caused the same evolution in Honolulu. The fire stations "each ... became powerful factors in the city's activities, even politically, and held their annual parades in February each year, an imposing procession of red-shirted, helmeted and capped men dragging their 'quaint' firefighting apparatus." Cartwright had been a vigorous participant in all the New York events, and he entered enthusiastically into the same sort of social and political activities now developing in Honolulu.

Of course, he remained as interested as ever in baseball, and it was natural that the fireman under his command absorbed his enthusiasm for the sport and that he turned to the fire station as a core component for the development of baseball teams. He had carried with him across the country a copy of his by-laws for baseball, along with one of the balls used by the Knickerbockers. The accommodating owner of the boot and shoe manufactory in Honolulu, J. H. Wood, was quite capable of fashioning leather or canvas-covered baseballs for Cartwright and the fireman. In accordance with Alick's revision of baseball that demanded force-outs at bases instead of plugging, the balls he now had made were harder and could be hit farther. We know that one such hard ball was used at the Punahou school, where flat bases were also a regular part of the game. Otherwise, it seems that before Alick arrived in Honolulu the Punahou players were still playing the older versions of rounders. Now that Cartwright brought his modern version of baseball to the islands, Hawaiians were on the cutting edge of the game in the 1850s. In particular, fire-fighting companies and baseball teams remained intimately associated. The firemen were responsible for creating the Association of Hawaii Baseball Clubs. Its meetings were held at the Hook & Ladder Company Hall, where the members of teams and the schedules were decided upon. Cartwright was starting over as a businessman, and also as the "Father of Baseball"—this time in Hawaii.

FREEMASONRY COMES TO HAWAII

Even as Cartwright's hopes for prosperity were being frustrated by the demise of the Bowlin and Cartwright company and the perfidy of the R. Coady company, he was achieving a personal reputation as a solid man through his effective conduct of the Fire Department and was becoming one of Hawaii's best-known residents. But firefighting was not the only activity that brought him into contact with the higher reaches of the Honolulu elites in business and government. He had achieved a reputation as a good organizer. So when business leaders decided to inaugurate a chamber of commerce in Honolulu, they knew at once that for the drafting of the by-laws and articles of incorporation the inevitable author was to be Alick. In due course he became the president of the Honolulu Chamber of Commerce.

The social activity that most engaged Alick early on was probably his membership in the Masons. The bent of his personality was always social. He was a joiner and from first to last a leader in social activities. Everything that he did showed evidence he enjoyed associating with others—in work, in play, in social fellowship. Not surprisingly, he had become a member of several social or fraternal clubs or societies in New York; among these he had already become a Master Mason before he left the city for California and Hawaii. Hardly had he settled in Hawaii when, on December 19, 1849, he petitioned the Honolulu lodge—Lodge Le Progress de l'Oceanie—for membership. The rather exotic title of this lodge is explained by the fact that when it was established in 1843, the prime mover in its foundation was Monsieur Le Tellier, who applied for admission of a lodge under a dispensation given by the Supreme Council of France. A French citizen, Tellier was captain of the bark *Ajax*, in whose cabin the first few meetings were conducted. Like many other American and European

Masonic lodges, members of the Honolulu unit were engaged in intellectual, free-thinking discussions of civic plans for the public good and the furtherance and preservation of enlightened reason in politics.

The lodge grew so rapidly that in 1851 Cartwright and a handful of other Master Masons met to consider forming a new lodge in Honolulu. The following year, the newly constituted "Hawaiian Lodge U.D." was granted a dispensation by the Grand Lodge of California. At the first regular meeting of the Hawaiian Lodge, on February 19, 1852, Cartwright was elected secretary, a sure sign that he was recognized as a reliable, moral, and orderly man. In the results of the first annual election in 1853, members of Hawaiian Lodge no. 21 voted to elect Cartwright "Senior Deacon." In subsequent years Cartwright "progressed through the chairs, skipping Senior Warden," and was elected Master for two terms, in 1855 and 1856.

Relations between the original lodge and the new one remained cordial, and Cartwright continued to participate enthusiastically in Masonic activities. On June 17, 1860, the two lodges joined together in the first public Masonic ceremony in the islands. On this occasion, they participated in the ritual of the laying of the cornerstone for the construction of the new Queen's Hospital, named after Queen Emma. By this time Cartwright had become the financial advisor to Emma, and he took a leading part in bringing the two lodges together on this occasion. Emma's husband, Kamehameha IV, still a member of the Le Progress Lodge, inevitably took the prime position of Grand Master of the event, but he was joined by Cartwright, who, representing Hawaiian Lodge No. 21, was elected as junior Grand Mason.

Cartwright remained active in the Masons throughout his life. For instance, in 1853, he successfully petitioned the Privy Council to remit the import duties on a ceremonial mace and Masonic regalia. In 1862, he organized a subscription fund to raise a monument to H. J. Poor, a deceased member of the lodge. The monument was to be constructed in California, which subjected it to duties upon its importation. Cartwright appealed to the Hawaiian minister of finance to waive the customs fees, and on September 10 the minister granted remission of duties. Cartwright even allied his Masonic enthusiasms to one of his hobbies. He collected Masonic medals from all over the world, eventually owning twenty of them.

His engagement with the Masonic institution and its ideals continued. In 1872, for instance, at the request of King Kamehameha V, a member of the Hawaiian Lodge, the cornerstone of the new government building was laid. With

Cartwright as Grand Master, the united Masons participated in this ceremony. Still later, in 1879, Alick would take major responsibility for raising the funds necessary to construct the first Masonic Hall in the islands. When the cornerstone was laid and the hall dedicated, he officiated on both occasions as Acting Grand Master. By this year, indeed, Cartwright had achieved legendary status among the Masons of Hawaii, since he was now the one survivor among those founders who were on the original roll of the lodge in 1852.

A GIFT FROM THE SEA—AND A LOSS

....

While Alick was struggling to keep Bowlin and Cartwright Company above water, then to make good at R. Coady & Co., to create and build a fire department, and to help the Freemasons of Hawaii flourish, another event occurred that both immeasurably eased his life and brought him new sorrow, perhaps the worst sadness he had yet experienced.

Alick's wife Eliza and his three children, DeWitt, Mary, and Catherine, left Boston on the *Eliza Warrick* in May 1851. By that time Alick was confident that he would be settling permanently in Hawaii. The trip was scheduled to try to ensure that the passengers would have warm weather and calm waters in the southern regions as they rounded Cape Horn during the southern summer, thence proceeding north along the west coast of Chile as the weather warmed in the northern hemisphere, to arrive in the Sandwich Islands sometime in January or even early February. The *Warrick* made a speedy journey, however, and arrived in Honolulu on December 1, 1851, five weeks earlier than expected. Alick met his family at the dock, paid Captain Watson $86.34 in additional freight charges, and happily brought his wife and children home to resume the life of a family man. His absence from his family had no doubt allowed him to plunge wholly into his many business, public, and social activities in Honolulu, and these had begun to win him esteem in commercial and governmental circles. But he had not seen his family since March 1, 1849, nearly three years before, when he had started his journey west. When Alick left New York, DeWitt Robinson was only five; now he was eight. Mary Groesbeck was three; now she was six. And he had never seen Catherine Lee, who had been conceived only a short time before his departure from New York. She was born just over seven months after Alick departed; now she would have been nearly a year and a half when the family docked in Honolulu.

Would have been—this was the sadness. Catherine Lee died aboard the

Warrick on November 16, 1851, two weeks before the ship docked in Honolulu. Her body was preserved, and Alick's first task upon greeting his family was to arrange for the burial of a child whom he had never seen alive.

From this time forward, some changes in Cartwright were noticeable. These were not entirely new tendencies but rather some old ones that deepened. First, always charitable and concerned for the welfare of others, Cartwright began to pay increased attention to children. Second, a strain of sadness came into his thinking. A man of action, he did not dwell in melancholy for long periods, but sadness now became an underlying strain of his personality. He could endure setbacks in business, for in his general optimism and self-confidence he seldom doubted that he would eventually prevail. But Catherine's death was irremediable, a blank wall of finality that could only be endured without hope. Nor would this be the last of his losses.

Alick expressed his new, underlying melancholy and his way of dealing with it in a letter to his sister Catherine, or "Kate," after whom little Catherine had been named. Catherine Cassio had written to him about her disappointments in life and recriminations concerning herself and others. In reply, he began, "My dear old Kate":

> You must not give way to sad thoughts and thus make yourself unhappy. When they intrude themselves, shake them off and busy yourself about your affairs. If you do not have any to busy yourself about, why then you must busy yourself about the affairs of others. Life is too short to spend it in vain regrets, and you must do as I do, determine to be jolly and shake off all unpleasant intrusions. Keep moving, keep busy. Body and mind must be constantly exercised or go stagnant.

Certainly, Alick took his own advice. He was known for his outward positivity and general optimism.

But in addition to the sadness that now tinged his life, there was also a noticeable increase in anxiety for his and others' children. One may hear a note of worry in 1853 when in writing to his friend Thomas Shillabee he mentions a current epidemic in Honolulu: "The small pox is raging violently among the natives (7 die out of 10) and although the whites have thus far escaped the contagion, it may be that they will not continue to do so, and in any case I would rather those I care for . . . [were] absent when pestilence stalks abroad over the land." Clearly, with the death of one child, the precariousness of life was apparent in a real way to him as it had never been before.

In 1852 Alick had only two surviving children. Not surprisingly, he turned his attention to his oldest child, his son, DeWitt Robinson, whose name was a constant reminder of his Knickerbockers teammate Peter DeWitt.

In 1852, DeWitt was nine years old—just the right age to be taught baseball. Alick often took long walks with his son, intent on imparting to him his own attitudes and interests. On one such walk they went all the way from downtown to the intersection of Keeaumoku and Kinau Streets where there was an open green space, undeveloped but already designated as "Makiki Park." Clearly, in going there, Cartwright had given some thought to this particular day and the direction of their stroll, for the park was some distance from their house. When they arrived, he started to talk to DeWitt about the Knickerbockers and the legendary games at Sunfish Pond and Elysian Fields. He reminisced about the time when he wrote out new rules to transform the old game of "townball" into baseball. Makiki Park was a pretty square field, and soon Alick took his son to the southwest corner and started to pace off a diamond, just as he had done in 1846 at Elysian Fields. He marked a home base: *This is where the batter starts.* Then he walked along the southern perimeter of the park: *Thirty paces.* With Cartwright's stride, that made ninety feet. He and DeWitt arrived at first base, turned at a right angle to the north, and walked off thirty paces, ninety feet again: *Second base, looking straight at home.* Left turn, thirty paces: third base; left for the last time, thirty paces, and there they were standing at "home" again: elementary geometry, perfect navigation. One more walk: start at home and walk fifteen paces directly toward second base; forty-five feet: *That is where the pitcher stands.* Now imagine foul lines stretching beyond the first and third base paths to the perimeter of the park. The field was completed;

the field of Cartwright's dreams had been paced out. Did he get DeWitt to run the bases? Very likely. Perhaps he had his old Knickerbocker ball in his pocket, the one he had played with during his cross-country journey. Were Alexander and DeWitt the first ones to play ball there? We do not know, but the imagination can save that as an alluring possibility. With little delay others would come and run these paths. The boys at Punahou followed Cartwright's plan and laid down their bases here at Makiki and were soon batting and running around Cartwright's field.

Once upon a time, in New York City, Alick had drawn up the first elaborate set of by-laws for a baseball club. He had taken the ball games that he knew and had played and revised and improved upon them and stuck some of their rules together and made a rule book for the new and improved game of baseball. Now, in Honolulu, he took the next step in the establishment of this sport. He laid out a field and subsequently he saw to it that baselines were drawn according to his plan. Bases were marked. The pitcher's box was situated. Once all that was done, Makiki Park magically became Makiki Field. And to this day it has remained a baseball field, only now it is named Cartwright Field.

On that spring day in 1852 Cartwright completed his invention of baseball. He laid out what was to become the oldest permanent baseball field anywhere in the world. One of Alick's business acquaintances later wrote that "Honolulu is one of the oldest baseball cities in the United States and has never, at any time, relinquished its special love of the national pastime. It is hard to conceive of a more rabid baseball city than Honolulu when we take into consideration the fact that Honolulu has more baseball clubs and leagues than any other city of like size."

Alexander Cartwright must be credited with stirring the passion for baseball in Hawaii. He did not bring baseball there first, but he did what he had done in New York—he brought a new conception of the game, and he created a field on which it could be played. With the arrival of his son and Alick's desire to impart to the boy his own passions, Cartwright, Peterson writes, was "rebitten by the bug" of baseball. After that day with DeWitt, he began to bring baseball to other children. Cartwright, Peterson says, "organized teams and taught the game all over the islands," with the result that "baseball was played widely in . . . Hawaii before it was introduced in half the area of the continental United States." While Cartwright did not by any means single-handedly introduce baseball to Hawaii, or see to its development entirely on his own, he was certainly involved in several ways with the ball game in the islands. Without question he remained as enthusiastic as ever over the sport he "fathered." Now, Cartwright's continuing contribution to the "invention" of baseball was as a public relations man, a "booster" of the game, as he went to various schools, drawing diamonds on the blackboard and proselytizing for his modern version of the game.

Cartwright's fourth child, Bruce, recalled his father's love of the game. Bruce, who was born in 1853, related how when he was a young boy in the 1860s,

> My father played [baseball] himself and was a "crank" up to the time of his death, never missing a game. His first and second right-hand fingers had been broken in playing. I remember well a little black book about five by three and one half inches with the word Knickerbocker in gold letters on the cover, which gave the rules of the game, bylaws, etc. of the original club of that name and of which he was the founder. I also remember a ball he brought across the plains. It was about four inches in diameter and very light. No human being could have thrown it over eighty yards. It was not a lively ball either. This was one of the first balls they ever played with.

Bruce was not the only person aware of Alick's baseball mania, which did indeed last until his death. In 1865 Cartwright wrote to his former Knickerbocker teammate Charles Deborst: "Charlie, I have in my possession the original ball with which we used to play on Murray Hill. Many an hour I have had [chasing] after it, on Mountain and Prairie, and many [on] an equally pleasant island home."

Soon after arriving in Honolulu, Cartwright became associated with the Punahou school, where baseball was important as a means to Americanizing natives and the offspring of the missionaries raised in the "foreign" Hawaiian land. At the school it was played by several of the faculty and most of the students. A student at Punahou, William Richards Castle, the son of Samuel Castle, one of the earliest missionaries, wrote in his *Reminiscences*:

> I used to have a good deal of business with Mr. Cartwright and while in his office one day . . . he surprised me by saying that he was an old ballplayer. . . . [His] interest seemed as keen and alive as ever and I remember seeing him out at Punahou several times, watching the play. He commented on some of the new features or different methods of playing.

Modest as always, Alick would not have said that he had been instrumental in designing some of the "new features or different methods of playing," though in speaking to Castle he did contrast "modern" baseball with the games he had learned as a young New Yorker. He had lost Catherine, but he had two living children and also still had his earliest creation—baseball—to teach to them and others. He followed the development of baseball on the mainland and was gratified to see that in 1858 it was his own old team, the Knickerbocker Baseball Club, whose "gentleman members" founded the "National Association of Amateur Baseball Players," incorporating into its regulations many of the components of Cartwright's by-laws. As he would counsel his sister Kate to do, he kept himself "busy" with these things. He kept himself busy for the rest of his life.

DEWITT AND HIS BROTHERS

C artwright had a strong wish to impart to his first son, DeWitt, a good education and his own values. When DeWitt reached the age of thirteen, Alick
decided that it was time to complete the boy's high school education. He located a school with a reliable headmaster, Mr. Hemenway, in Sheffield, Connecticut, and enrolled DeWitt there for the fall semester of 1856. Writing to
Hemenway of his aspirations for DeWitt's progress there, he began: "I am most
anxious that he should become a *good* businessman"—Cartwright intention-
ally stressed *good*, and he continued in this vein, hoping that DeWitt "should
become a man of noble principles, generous mind, and enlarged views." On the
following day, he wrote more fully to DeWitt himself, enclosing a letter from
DeWitt's sister, Mary Groesbeck, and another from one of DeWitt's Honolulu
friends. Cartwright used these as guides to illustrate exemplary, responsible
behavior in all things, advising DeWitt that he must be punctilious in answering
letters and be especially attentive to the individual interests of his correspon-
dents. "Don't be afraid of your time, labor, or paper," he urged his son. Finally,
he turned to loving advice: "study hard, take plenty of exercise, be obedient
to your teacher and elders, kind and generous to your schoolmates, affable
to all." The consistency with which Cartwright urged on his son self-reliance
fused with responsibility to others illumines the core of his own personality.
In subsequent letters to his faraway boy he continued to stress promptness,
consideration, and reliability. He told DeWitt that he himself was "toiling night
and day" to make sufficient money to educate his children. Always, he stressed
the acquisition of good habits: "Be a good boy. Attend strictly . . . to your studies—and obey your teacher in all things."

Dewitt's summer vacations from school presented a problem. The arduous and lengthy trip from Connecticut to Honolulu did not allow the boy to make a round trip home and back to school during a single summer. But, of course, there was still a sizable Cartwright contingent in New York, and DeWitt spent his long vacations at Kate Cassio's house. "Please write me how you are pleased with DeWitt," Alick would inquire anxiously of his family concerning DeWitt's progress in education and behavior. In his usual tenderhearted way, he yearned to see the boy. "Don't forget to get[,] to send the Photographs[,] all you can get[,] of the family and DeWitt," Cartwright would beg of Kate and George Cassio.

By 1857, Alick and Eliza had two more children. Bruce was born on November 16, 1853, about two years after Eliza arrived in Honolulu. Then, on February 26, 1855, Eliza gave birth to Alexander Joy Cartwright III. With DeWitt away at school, there were still three Cartwright children at home in 1857. Now Alick yearned to tell his family in New York how wonderful his two new little boys were. "Bruce is a beauty," he wrote, but Alexander III "beats them all." To George Cassio he added: "I wish [my] mother could see Alexander, Jr. He is just the finest fellow that ever crowed [i.e., lived] and a beauty too."

Alick spoke the truth when he said that he was "toiling night and day." Having finally made a separation from Richard Coady, he was striking out in several directions. Honolulu was at the center of an economically burgeoning society; there was plenty of opportunity, along with an equal amount of risk. Like his earliest mentor, Howe, Cartwright took the path of "safety in numbers" and had many irons in the fire, reasoning that if one failed, another would prosper. He avidly sought out new opportunities. He heard some rumors that an insurance agency might become available because of the poor work of the current agent, and in 1853 he told George Cassio that he was ready to seize the possibility. To juggle many different prospects and to take chances on them requires a good deal of self-confidence, and Alick had it. To George, he added that he was as well qualified for the office as any other man in the Islands. In fact, Cartwright did get the agency. In late 1853, he secured a commission as an insurance agent for the New York Board of Underwriters, writing policies for commercial shippers. He added a life-insurance component to this by way of New York Equitable Life Insurance Company. Finally, in his steady, accumulative way, he extended the agency to include fire insurance. Since he was the fire chief, that part of his insurance business rapidly flourished. To be sure, these brought little income at the outset, but they signaled the beginning of the active program he would follow.

His work, as he told DeWitt, was done for the sake of the family. For the family, too, he had to find suitable housing. Before the arrival of Eliza and the children he had rented a house at the junction of Alakea, Union, and Beretania Streets. Now he wanted a new residence, one large enough for his family. But building in Hawaii had not kept pace with the demand, and the housing market was tight. For over a year, he had had his eye on a fine house situated at Fort and Chaplain Streets. This one-story, cottage-style house had been built in 1849 by F. W. Thompson, the leading auctioneer in 1840s Honolulu, and was still owned by his widow. The house was elegantly designed. Indeed, it was one of those illustrated in an engraving showing the most attractive residences in early Honolulu in the *Hawaiian Annual of 1899*.

He got the house, which was situated with easy access to the downtown waterfront, and close enough to Punahou that the children could attend school there. At the same time, in 1853, there was a "building boom" in Honolulu, especially in commercial real estate. In this boom, as one historian writes, "there occurred the inauguration of larger and better business structures than any that had preceded." Among these prominent structures was the twin building of Swan & Clifford on Queen Street at the foot of Kaahumanu, which was long to remain a prominent structure and landmark on the waterfront. The historian of building progress in Honolulu, Thomas Thrum, writes: "Upon its completion, Mr. A. J. Cartwright moved into [it] and occupied the Waikiki-side of the second story, while the U.S. Consulate was located on the Ewa-side."

And so by the end of 1853 Cartwright had settled the questions of his domestic residence and business location. He remained in this home for a long time and opened his own office in the distinguished downtown building, where he was in close proximity to Swan & Clifford, ship chandlers. This firm was well capitalized and growing rapidly, and Cartwright, for his part, by this time had plentiful experience in this very business. Soon he began to take on overflow work from Swan & Clifford.

Cartwright had been newcomer to Hawaii in 1849, but within four years he had built a solid reputation. His work at Coady & Co. was respected. He was chief engineer (or fire chief) of the Honolulu Fire Department. During his time in Lahaina he had established good contacts with the whaling fleets and was doing insurance underwriting for East Coast whalers and local and mainland shippers. His experience as a ship chandler as far back as his work with Howe equipped him to share in the business of Swan & Clifford. His prominent membership in the Masons brought him good social contacts. None of these varied activities, of course, was done merely for success. The simple fact was that Cartwright plunged into the new Hawaiian world, and it found places for him. Among earlier Americans he resembles no one so much as Benjamin Franklin. Like Franklin in Philadelphia, he joined an unformed society and sought to make it work through political reform and compromise, public works, private charities, and, in general, in Franklin's phrase, "doing good." Like Franklin he was a pragmatist, endlessly in search of what worked in his community, whether in baseball or public works, government, educational institutions, or commerce.

Cartwright, of course, had occasional doubts about whether he had made the right choice in staying in Hawaii. The death of his daughter, Catherine Lee, left him with some recriminations. Wouldn't she still be alive if he had stayed in New York? Besides, his older brother Ben, who had remained in New York City, was making a solid success there. Even after he had Eliza and the children to come to the islands, he was not entirely sure that he had made the right decision to settle in Honolulu. In June 1853 he mused to a friend whom he had made during his brief stays in San Francisco that perhaps he should have stayed there: "How much I wish that business would call me to San Francisco. . . . I long once more to see the friends I've left behind. Memory oft recurs to those few happy months. . . . I think of them all with pleasure. I know not why unless it is that friends, dear friends, were there." Of course, many of his Knickerbocker teammates had settled in the city. Even as late as 1872, Cartwright still considered leaving Hawaii. He wrote to Richard I. Howland, a San Francisco friend: "I have thought seriously of acting upon your advice and transferring my business to San Francisco, but upon consideration have decided to wait another year, to see if this business is likely to continue, and also to see if it will continue at San Francisco."

In 1876, when the Centenary of the Declaration of Independence was to be celebrated in Philadelphia, he felt a strong, patriotic urge to celebrate with his fellow Americans. He became one of three Hawaiian citizen members of the Committee of Finance to raise funds for the celebration. As early as 1873, he spoke with other U.S. citizens in Hawaii about attending the upcoming centenary. John Dominis talks of going, he wrote: "Should he go, it is just possible that I may come with him. In any event, 1876—deo volante—I [will] go to Philadelphia." Still, he did not leave Hawaii. When it was too late to depart for

Philadelphia, in June 1876, he and others prepared "to celebrate the 'Centennial' in a small way—and propose to fire powder enough on the 4th to make the Kanakas realize that [patriotism] . . . still lives." As always, taking the optimistic view, he concluded that "many of our good folks are off to the 'little affair' in Philadelphia, who in after years will have to regret that they did not stay home and see our part of the show."

Seemingly the single most important factor to have strengthened Cartwright's resolve to settle in Honolulu was the example of his brother Alfred de Forest. Alfred simply couldn't decide where to settle and what business to settle on. The result was that he made no headway at all as he moved from San Francisco to Honolulu and back again. Alfred's Honolulu venture with Alick's former partner Richard Bowlin also failed when Bowlin, always at loose ends, decided to depart for San Francisco, where he died. Alfred then moved back to San Francisco and allied with new partners, but he did no better there. In 1854, Alick heard through Richard Coady that in San Francisco Alfred was in great distress and did not know what to do, feeling that everybody had deserted him. Alick lent him $200 and wrote Alfred several times, but Alfred was deep in depression and never answered. Alick located possible work for Alfred in Honolulu, "which may result in something to his advantage." He told George Cassio that he would happily take Alfred into his home but could do little else and was unable to pay Alfred's debts in San Francisco. Still, Alick subsequently scraped up the $200 to send, but it was hard to do even that. Told by their mother that Alick was succeeding grandly in Honolulu, Alfred again applied to Alick for help. Alick wrote back ruefully: "I am very sorry that you have not succeeded better, but the old adage that a 'rolling stone gathers no moss' is exemplified in your case, as it has in many others." As to their mother's sunny appraisal, Alick added, "I am tight for money . . . things are awfully dull here. My business is at a dead standstill." The only advice he could give was that Alfred should cut expenses.

Alfred returned to Honolulu in late July 1856 on the ship *Francis Palmer* to make a try at the work that Alick had found for him. "Alfred has just arrived," Alick wrote in a letter back to the family in New York, and he assured them that "I shall employ him until I can find something better for him to do. I gave him $1000 and his board[,] equal to $1500 per annum. It's more than I can afford." In 1859, Alfred finally opened a family grocery and feed store on Ford Street in Odd Fellows Hall. Alick actually funded the store but the sign above the door read "A. D. Cartwright Feedstore." This was the first feed store in Honolulu, and it seemed sure of success. Alfred's wife, Rebecca, and their child had recently gone back to New York from California, and so Alfred lived with Alick and his family on nearby Fort Street from 1856 to 1858. Contrary to all expectations, the grocery and feed store did not prosper, and Alfred was soon at loose ends again. So, Alfred Cartwright continued to be a "rolling stone." Even as late as 1883, he was still passing back and forth between California and Hawaii. In that year he told Alick he would come to Honolulu "to settle." But it was too late, for as Alick told Kate, "his chances would not be good" for "this place is overstocked with people of all nations seeking business or employment." Nonetheless, Alick was ever ready to help his brother, and he told Alfred, "I hold the agency for the Equitable Life Assurance Society and would pass it over to you" if Alfred wanted it. But Alfred vacillated to the end.

By contrast, Alexander Cartwright stayed in Hawaii, as in 1873 he predicted he would: "the old ones . . . cling to Hawaii nei, and will probably end our days here. And why not as well here as anywhere?"

CARTWRIGHT & CO., LTD.

A lick prospered. The groundwork of reliability that he laid down proved a good foundation upon which to build a business success.

When he left R. Coady & Co. for good, he continued to supply whalers. Some newspaper accounts of the time call him "a shipping and whaling agent." While still working at Coady's he had independently become the sole agent for the Association of Cold Springs (Long Island) Whaleships. He carried on this relation with them after he left Coady's and also developed an exclusive and friendly commercial relation with the captains of the whaling fleet from New Bedford, Massachusetts. His correspondence with such whaling captains as William H. Vinal, Martin Palmer, David B. Nye, William F. Dan Epps, and William F. Dow, along with whale ship owners, such as Edward C. Jones, was extensive. The names of such whaling vessels as the *Sheffield*, the *Yankee*, the *Hibernia*, and the schooner *Rialto*, dot his business files. To facilitate his source of supply, he developed a relation with another ship chandler in Honolulu, Wilcox, Richards & Co., beginning in 1859 and extending to the mid-1860s. For them, he was not an employee but an independent commission agent. At first he was quite dependent on the whaling industry, as, indeed, Honolulu as a whole was. Cartwright called it a "one horse town," and he worried for himself about his economic dependence upon the fleet. "Should the Whaling Fleet fall off from any cause," he moaned, "we must all emigrate or starve." Nonetheless, his fears were always lessened by his personal optimism and his confidence in his friendly relations with the whalers. "I have been most fortunate in having so many friends among the Masters," he said flatly. "I am not ambitious," he wrote to his friend Arthur M. Ebberts Epps, but "if my good friends the whalers will enable me to earn an honest livelihood and add a few hundred per annum to my little capital, I will [be] well content."

Cartwright's business with the whalers became double-pronged when, in addition to supplying them, he expanded his insurance business to insuring whaling ships. He became a member of the National Board of Marine Underwriters, New York.

He further extended his shipping concerns by beginning to look for articles that could be imported from the mainland and profitably sold in Hawaii. In 1850 he had made his first success by exporting food to the mainland. In five short years Hawaii had grown rapidly, and now he turned to importing. He asked a relative in New York for help with suggestions concerning manufactured articles and general merchandise and promised to make as quick a sale as any merchant in Honolulu. Specifically, he added that wines and liquors, tobacco, and all sorts of groceries would find a good market in Honolulu. As the former fire chief, too, he began to insure against fires through the Imperial Fire Insurance Co. of London. Cartwright's diversified business was being built piece by piece. As he once said of it, his business was "made up of a thousand details." Now his company was called, simply, Cartwright and Co., Ltd.

ALEXANDER JOY CARTWRIGHT JR., AMERICAN

One of the remarkable features of Alexander Cartwright's life is his passionate Americanness. Once he decided to make his life in Honolulu, he plunged into its economic, cultural, social, and educational life. He even learned the Hawaiian language, as his correspondence indicates. He conducted business in it and expanded his social contacts through it. But he never applied for Hawaiian citizenship, as many other United States citizens did, many even marrying native Hawaiians as a way to gain influence with the native rulers. Indeed, an article written about Cartwright noted in particular that he was a fervent patriot: "So strong . . . are his love for and his loyalty toward the land of his birth, that he has refused to take the [Hawaiian] oath of allegiance, even in times past when it was, more than now, advisable for those having business interests in this country, to become Hawaiian citizens." He spoke of the United States as "my beloved country" and remained steadfastly an American. In 1857 he wrote to a Mr. Muir: "I still think New York the only city in the world, and I am still an American citizen . . . and all the offices and all the wealth of the Islands would not tempt me to forfeit my allegiance to Uncle Sam. I am one of the liveliest Americans ever you saw and celebrate . . . all the 4th of Julys." He was not exaggerating. He maintained a very lively and informed interest in the doings of the United States and in the welfare of American citizens visiting Hawaii or living there. In the 1850s he founded the American Relief Fund, which had as its object the assistance of needy Americans in Hawaii. He was its first treasurer and eventually its president. He was also an early member of the patriotic American Club and an avid participant in the celebration of America on national holidays. For Washington's birthday in 1857, for instance, he addressed the members of the American Club and invited Prince Lot Kamehameha to assist the club in the celebration. He persuaded Lot to lend the government's artillery to the American Club and began the celebration of the day with a roar of cannons. Cartwright began a sentence to a friend in New York City, "Ardent Republican as I am," and he indicated later to his son that "as I am an American it makes little difference to me who is 'king' in Hawaii." With regard to "His Majesty Kalakaua," Cartwright "thanked God" that he was not one of his subjects.

Cartwright also paid close attention to events on the mainland. When he learned that a statue was to be erected by public subscription to the general of the Army of the Tennessee, James Birdseye McPherson, killed in the Civil War before Atlanta, Georgia, he became immediately interested. At once, he sent $200, asking that the sum be applied toward the erection of a monument to mark McPherson's last resting place. When the funds for the monument were raised, he wrote to Secretary of State William H. Seward with "thanks . . . for the patriotic interest you evinced in the fame of one of their distinguished citizens who battled for the life of the nation."

Cartwright had no personal interest in McPherson, who was from Ohio. But he was keenly interested, even at this distance, in his native land. When the great Midwestern fires swept the nation in 1871, he immediately donated money for the relief of the inhabitants of Illinois, Minnesota, and Wisconsin, sending a draft of $1,500 to W. C. Ralston of the Bank of California for the victims. To the mayor of Milwaukee he sent $379, which he collected from the managers of Castle and Company. George M. Pullman—the maker of the renowned "Pullman cars"—was treasurer of the Chicago Relief Aid Society and sent out a circular letter pleading for assistance. Cartwright responded by sending money he had collected from local businesses and prominent citizens: Charles R. Bishop ($50), S. N. Castle ($25), A. J. Cartwright ($50), J. H. Black ($10), Dillingham Co. ($15), and J. C. Pfluger ($100). In January 22, 1872, Cartwright complained that "business is very dull" but "not withstanding our own losses, [we] can find time (and a little money) to sympathize with our suffering fellow creatures in Chicago and Wisconsin."

These are but two of many instances of how closely Cartwright followed the American scene and how passionately he involved himself in it. Cartwright's stubborn refusal to give up his American citizenship was certainly noticed and commented on or wondered about. An article written about him in the last year of his life pointedly stated: "Mr. Cartwright has been often importuned to become an Hawaiian citizen and accept political office, but this he has always refused to do, on account of his pro-American sentiments."

The *Pacific Commercial Advertiser* gave an accurate picture of Cartwright in 1892, citing his "liberal views" and his "earnest" support of "any measure conducive to [Hawaii's] political welfare," but stressing Cartwright's Americanism: "We think it not too much to say," the editor wrote, "that in case Hawaii were to become a portion of the United States, no man in the Kingdom would be more pleased than would A. J. Cartwright." (A mere six years later, Hawaii came under U.S jurisdiction.) In sum, the editor wrote, though Cartwright took a "deep interest" in "the progress of [Hawaii], he is, nevertheless, an enthusiastic American of genuine Yankee Stock." His "Americanism" was obviously well known since another article stated, "Perhaps his most sterling trait was his conspicuous patriotism—a stalwart American of the old Henry Clay school of 1840, and this trait endeared him to every American, whether Republican or Democrat."

Cartwright's life offers a strong corrective to the portrait of the American businessman during the period of 1840 through 1900 that we have inherited from the works of major novelists of this period. Each in his or her own way, such writers as Henry James, William Dean Howells, Henry Adams, Edith Wharton, and Theodore Dreiser convey a picture of, on the one hand, overworked, regretful, uncultured, lonely, unfulfilled entrepreneurs or, on the other, rapacious, grasping, greedy captains of industry who seek power and domination. Each of the major writers of the period attempted to define the businessman type—and the picture each produced was largely negative.

Henry Adams's *Chapters of Erie* (1871) is one of the earliest critiques of the corruption in business and the decline of idealism that followed the Civil War. Adams found that the political world and business life in America under the Grant administration "are gloriously rich and stink like hell." Later, in *The Education of Henry Adams* (1907), he portrays the American entrepreneur as either grimly staying at his desk or else listlessly following in the wake of a relentless wife as she scours Europe for more and more culture to consume. Howells's best known novel, *The Rise of Silas Lapham* (1885) offers a dark portrait of the new businessman. Dryfoos, recently a farmer, becomes a power on the New York Stock Exchange after the discovery of oil on his property. Howells's main character, Basil March, sees that the man has "undergone a moral deterioration in succeeding. All of his generous instincts have been turned toward money-making." He becomes a pitiless social Darwinist.

The portrait becomes darker as time passes. Such Edith Wharton novels as *The House of Mirth* (1905) are full of the newly rich—Gus Trenor, Simon

Rosedale, Elmer Moffat—whose lives are limited to conquest, power, and material acquisition. This character type is brought to a vehement fulfillment in Dreiser's Trilogy of Desire: *The Financier* (1912), *The Titan* (1914), and *The Stoic* (1947), concerning the real magnate Samuel Yerkes, whom Dreiser called "a rebellious Lucifer."

The title and epigraph for my biography of Alexander Joy Cartwright Jr. come from Henry James, who portrayed the American businessman as a tireless drudge at work, who only too late comes to Europe and catches a glimpse of the life he has lost. In *The American* (1871), Christopher Newman is "fabulously rich" but suddenly experiences a "moral disgust" with business and arrives in Europe, where he discovers all that he has missed. It is Lambert Stether in *The Ambassadors* (1903) who best typifies the lost American businessman. He gives the melancholy advice to a young man: "Live all you can." To the end of his career, in the unfinished novel *The Ivory Tower* (1917), James was still writing about the difficulty of escaping from the illusion that money or sensuality can produce a full life.

Strether never did live all he could; his knowledge came too late. But Alexander Joy Cartwright Jr. did. Of course, he experienced the sadness, losses, and disappointments common to all lives. But he lived life to the full in New York and Honolulu. In love for his family, in charitable and social activities, in a swirl of business ventures, and in his lifelong passion for baseball, he seized every chance offered him for joy in living. Above all, more than any of the created characters of the major American novelists of his time, he reveled in being an American. Happy and fulfilled persons do not lend themselves to dramatic fiction. They are, as Tolstoy wrote, boringly "all alike." The period of 1840 through 1897 was itself as dramatic and "interesting" a time of change and experiment as anyone could want. Cartwright swam rather happily in the currents of his vital, progressive age, and his life gives us a more accurate picture of the successful man of his time than any of the major novelists did.

THE SOCIAL WHIRL

C artwright's refusal to take the oath of allegiance to become a Hawaiian citizen did not retard or reverse his steady progress toward social standing, commercial prosperity, or political influence. During the 1860s through the 1880s his efforts came to a full flowering as he steadily built upon the foundation of reliability that he had established in the 1850s. But Cartwright had another side to his life beside business. He participated richly in the growing cultural and social life in Honolulu. Indeed, he was a major contributor to the creation of culture and civilization there. In less than thirty years Honolulu was transformed from a backwater city of commerce and grass huts to a city of fine buildings and a budding civilization. A visitor to the city in 1882 was surprised to see that with "regard to the public taste of Honolulu, I may say that the bon ton of the best society is in no inferior order, and that it improves considerably with every year; that the spirit of the higher social classes is pervading, to a wonderful extent, the whole life of the city."

His standing in society can be partly seen in the diary that his second daughter, Mary Groesbeck Cartwright, wrote during her seventeenth year, between August 26, 1862, and July 7, 1863. Her life consisted of one social or cultural occasion after the other. She had many friends whom she visited regularly or from whom she received frequent visits. In her diary she gives accounts of calling upon members of the most prominent families in Honolulu, such as the Bishops and their children. She writes of parties, dances, and games. She records her regular attendance at church and social occasions. She tells of her studies of French and German and of her reading. She is especially enthusiastic about her growing skill on the piano—and even writes down a list of forty-two pieces of sheet music in her possession. She belongs, too, to a singing society and has many friends in it. The picture that she gives is that the Cartwrights moved easily in Hawaiian society. Her father, of course, had an even wider social life. "The town," he wrote in 1875, "is gay with balls, parties, & c." He gave a brief account: "Our little town is . . . very lively for pleasure . . . today a dinner at Mr. Pierces, tomorrow evening a ball at [U.S.A.] Minister Grews, Wednesday a Dinner at the Hotel of our Laird MacGregor, a wealthy Scotchman, Thursday reception on board the 'Pensacola,' Friday ball at Hawaiian Hotel . . . Saturday concert at the Theatre." The theater was a particular interest for Cartwright. He was a leading member of the committee that in 1888 began to raise funds to build the Music Hall. He saw his efforts realized in the erection of a "fine brick building." Daniel E. Bandmann, a British actor who gave several performances at the theater, described it in 1882: "The theatre in Honolulu is far beyond the requirements of the city, and worthy of any first-class provincial town in the world."

Alick belonged to many clubs, such as the Honolulu Rifles, the Maile Club, the Pacific, the Commercial, and the American Club, in addition to the Masons. He attended numerous birthday dinners throughout the year. He attended each king's birthday dinner annually. He was a trustee of the Music Hall Association of Honolulu. He sponsored and arranged for balls on special occasions. For instance, for Honolulu's first formal ball, held in 1853 at the Merchant's Exchange building, he is listed as one of the "managers" of the affair, along with such well-known community leaders as W. B. Rice and M. C. Monsarrat. He regularly attended the book auctions held by Monsarrat. Records exist of the purchases he made of such serious books as Bunyan's *Pilgrims Progress* and such poetry as James Thomson's *The Seasons*, Longfellow's *Evangeline*, Poe's *The Raven*, and many others. He was especially interested in mythology and owned books on Greek, Native American, American, Russian, and Norse myths. He read biographies avidly, including volumes on Louis XIV, Marie de Medici, and Oliver Cromwell. Cartwright helped to found the Honolulu Library and Reading Room and was named to its first board of directors, a post he kept from 1880 to his death in 1892. Indeed, he donated from his own collections most of the library's first 200 books. "Mr. Cartwright was always, until his death, a generous donor to the Library," a commentator on the development of the library wrote.

Cartwright's participation in the cultural life of Honolulu took a surprising turn in 1884 when he and Godfrey Rhodes lent the *Daily Hawaiian* newspaper $4,000 to keep its doors open. Cartwright was already an investor in the paper—he owned $500 in shares. But by April 1885 the directors defaulted on the loan and he came into possession of the paper. Unfortunately, the paper failed, and Cartwright and Rhodes seized its property and foreclosed.

Cartwright also helped to found churches and contributed financially to build them. He was widely involved in local charities. Records exist of his sending money to Father Damien for support of the leper colony, of his personal support of orphaned children and destitute widows, and of his relief efforts on behalf of needy men, down on their luck. He even turned one of his hobbies into social occasions. Cartwright, a newspaper account of this life noted, was "an enthusiast on the subject of numismatics, and has a really magnificent collection of ancient and modern coins. . . . These are systematically arranged for convenient reference in cabinets, and are one of the attractions of his charming home." Anyone interested in the display in Cartwright's home museum was welcome to visit him and inspect the collection.

Another part of Cartwright's social life came from a surprising quarter. He represented two Latin American countries, Chile and Peru, as consul and head of the legation. This means that he became a member of the consular board in Honolulu and was an important figure in the business of international trade with the islands. He had learned Spanish while still a young man in New York. In 1865, he became acting consul for Peru and soon after became permanent consul. As a consequence, he was invited to social gatherings at all the consulates on the occasions of their national holidays. In 1886, he was appointed acting consul to Hawaii for Chile. He served as consul for Peru for sixteen years, and his work was so excellent that at his death his son Bruce succeeded him in the position. For Alick, the two consular positions placed him in the company of the representatives of many foreign nations and kept him abreast of cultural and economic developments on the international scene. Among his papers are numerous invitations to events sponsored by the consulates and the government of Hawaii. He always attended the Fourth of July parties at the American legation, but as a consul he was always also invited to important events at all the legations. For instance, in 1867 he went to the British consulate in May to celebrate the birthday of Queen Victoria. So it went all through the year, and year after year Cartwright's life was lived in a whirl of internationalism.

Cartwright's business ventures continued to prosper. With such a wide net of civic, consular, charitable, governmental, and social activities and acquaintances, even a moderately able businessmen would inevitably gain a respectable success. But Cartwright was a superb businessman, careful, reliable, honest, and thoughtful. He became a master of business involving native disputes and became fluent in the Hawaiian language necessary to settle them. He conducted a lively business and philanthropic correspondence in Hawaiian. No wonder he was sought out to serve on boards and to administer not just estates but major companies. He was the first president of the Hawaiian Stock Exchange and was appointed president of the Union Iron Works, helping to put the company on a firm financial footing.

But the business activity that brought together all of Cartwright's other activities was his representation of the interests of Hawaii's Queen Emma.

ADVISOR TO THE QUEEN

F ollowing the death of her husband, King Kamehameha IV, Queen Emma Kaleleonalani necessarily relied on her properties and the income from them for financial support, to supplement her continuing royal perquisites.

But Emma's possessions were in a muddle: deeds had been lost, property lines were confused, and rents were not being duly collected. What was needed most was an administrator whose honesty could be trusted, whose executive and accounting skills were of the highest order, who knew the customs of and the people involved in the Privy Council, who understood the Hawaiian language (since most of the documents and deeds were in the original language), whose business connections were broad, and who, finally, had adequate energy to undertake the task of getting everything in order. Alick had begun administrating estates as early as 1862, and it was apparent that Cartwright was the very person to put Emma's estate in order. He had been associated with the queen ever since he became involved with her in founding the Queen's Hospital. Indeed, it was Alick who helped to draw up the charter and by-laws of the hospital, founded "for relief of indigent, sick, and disabled people of the Hawaiian kingdom." After the hospital was built he was appointed a trustee in 1863 and served in that position for four years.

In 1874, he became Queen Emma's advocate and advisor and began to bring some clarity to her holdings. He signed himself officially as her "Attorney in Fact." As early as January 1875, he informed Rufus A. Lyman, the land commissioner for the Hawaiian Islands, that he was undertaking to represent Queen Emma in the question of the boundaries of lands given to her by royal patent or personal acquisition, and that he intended to begin working on her properties on the big island of Hawaii by doing land surveys of them. In February, he hired a surveyor, D. H. Hitchcock, who referred to Cartwright as "Agent for Queen Emma." By August 17, 1875, he was able to give a report to His Excellency Paul Nahaolelua Lahaina:

> I have got all the lands of Emma registered in a book with the titles and everything complete, that is in the event of an accident to me, everything concerning the Estate would be found in plain and perfect order. . . . I find in Emma's matters there has been a great deal of careless neglect, lands have been suffered to lie still that should have been leased or sold, thus losing much money. In many cases the title is imperfect, or incomplete, several valuable lands are held in the original award and have never been patented. . . . [Other] lands have never been surveyed and avaricious neighbors are constantly trying to steal something from their true boundaries. It is my present intention to have all these lands properly surveyed and their bounds fixed by the boundary commission, so that hereafter there shall be no dispute concerning them.

Cartwright proceeded efficiently: Hitchcock soon completed the several surveys. The boundaries were filed with the land commissioners, and Alick began to turn what had been profitless properties into cash by renting out Emma's lands, acting as agent to collect the rents, and finally by paying the taxes on the resulting profits. Soon Hawaiian entrepreneurs were busily engaged in contacting Cartwright to arrange to rent the properties that were now, finally, available for development. "I noticed in the papers," Valdemar Knudsen wrote to Cartwright, "that you have the management of Queen Emma's affairs"; he, like many others, sought to lease her lands. By 1877, Alick had achieved some clarity over the properties in the island of Hawaii, and he proceeded to establish the boundaries of land at Halehaku and Opana in Maui. Interior Department documents show that as late as 1885 Cartwright was engaged in protecting the interest of Emma's estate. In February of that year, he sued the Honolulu Water Works for damage to her land at Makiki and on another property at Fort and Hotel Streets, and he succeeded in getting awards of $4,615 for the two. Until he died in 1892, Cartwright continued to administer the estate. The task of clarifying boundaries on old patents was always confusing, arduous, and extremely time-consuming, but Cartwright vigorously persisted over the decades. For instance, he attempted to get a decision on boundaries on some of Emma's lands in Waimea in Maui, and he got a title certificate from Judge

Robertson there after a long investigation. But the boundary remained nearly as indefinite then as it had been at the beginning. Natives on the property, Alick was informed, all said that Judge Robertson's boundary was in the middle of the land, and there remained a dispute as to the boundary at the seashore between Emma's land and Kanai hae. Finally, Land Commissioner Lyman had to investigate and issue a decision himself—in Emma and Cartwright's favor. But there were always innumerable such disputes to get settled.

As evidence of Emma's gratitude to Cartwright in 1875, she conveyed to him a parcel of her land at Waikiki, where he soon built a house and made his second residence away from the city. Indeed, Emma continued to be so profoundly grateful to Alick that in her will she made a provision that Cartwright's "heirs and assigns [shall] be forever the executers of her estate." The estate continues to be administered by Cartwright and Sons to the present day.

Of course, Alick's work on behalf of Queen Emma helped to create and extend business for him as a land agent, real estate advisor, and manager of estates. In the course of dealing with her estate, he became something of an expert on boundaries and titles and especially on the important questions of water rights. Eventually he became executor and trustee of numerous wills and estates. He was often appointed an arbitrator concerning land titles. Most important of all, through his work on Emma's affairs, he subsequently became financial advisor to King Kamehameha V, to elected King Luanulilo (1873–1874), and then to King Kalakaua, until the latter's death in 1891. He not only spoke and wrote the Hawaiian language, he was given a Hawaiian name, U Moe O A. J. Kahalaeka. In 1883, he received a remarkable appointment, recorded in an official document of state:

> Know . . . that we, Kalakaua, of the Hawaiian Islands, King, and Kapiolani his wife for her right of dower, Lilioukalani K. Dominis and John D. Dominis her husband, Miriam Likelike Cleghorn, and Archibald J. Cleghorn, her husband, . . . do hereby severally make, constitute and appoint Alexander J. Cartwright and Charles H. Judd . . . our true, sufficient and lawful attorneys, for us, in our names, and to our use and benefit, to lease and collect the rents and to sell and convey for such price as they may think fit, all of our right title and interest.

This meant, in effect, that the royal land holdings came under the control and disposal of Cartwright and Judd, making them among the most powerful people in the kingdom. And finally, for a year, until he himself died, Cartwright was the advisor to Queen Lilioukalani, eventually the last of the Hawaiian monarchs to rule.

But Cartwright, in his invariable democratic way, dealt with simple and unfortunate people equally with kings and queens. Among his papers may be found several letters much like one in 1880, when he handled the lease "to Amana the Chinaman" of land belonging to "the little orphan Stella who owns the land." Indeed, he had made a vow, he told his sister Esther, to "consider myself personally responsible for all investments made by me for accounts of widows and orphans." He guaranteed that they would not lose any money though his investments and promised a minimum of a 9 percent dividend.

Cartwright's Americanism and his democratic spirit showed up unfailingly in all his actions. His efforts on behalf of Queen Emma or "little orphan Stella" were given with equal integrity and commitment. His tirelessness and his American capacity for invention and organization showed in his business endeavors no less than in his invention of baseball. Though in distant Hawaii, he was participating in the creation of a distinctive American character, a "new man" on the global stage.

Yet while he was striving to make his businesses successful, Alick was experiencing personal sadness.

In April, 1871, Cartwright's father died. Alick urged his mother to relocate to Honolulu and spend the remainder of her life in Hawaii, declaring himself "most happy to give her a home," but she remained with her daughters in New York. Alick continued the $200 annual contribution that he had sent his parents since 1861. He also renounced his portion of his inheritance and assigned it to his sister Kate. Alick's brother Benjamin died six years later, on the August 12, 1877, after a lingering illness. These deaths might have been expected, but not those of his children.

The mortality rate was high in Hawaii. Numerous exotic diseases arrived with the ships that docked in Honolulu from all over the world and with the increasing numbers of immigrants, first from China and then from Japan and the Philippines. This was the largest cause of the steady decline of the native population. But Europeans were nearly as vulnerable as Hawaiians to diseases from the Far East to which they had never been exposed.

The two children who had survived the voyage around Cape Horn on the *Eliza Warrick*, DeWitt Robinson and Mary Groesbeck, both died at an early age. Mary was the first to go. She died on June 4, 1869, three days after her twenty-fourth birthday. Three years earlier she had married Alfred Godley Frederick Maitland. The marriage failed, and shortly after their separation, she died of scarlet fever, "sine prodige," as Cartwright wrote, unable to give an expression to his grief except in a foreign language. Nine months later, on March 20, 1870, DeWitt perished at the age of twenty-six. Family legend has it that he was poisoned. All three of the children that Alick and Eliza brought into the world in New York were in graves in Honolulu. In expressing sympathy for the grief over a loss in a friend's family, Cartwright, in a rare personal statement, wrote of his own grief and consolation: "I have had more than my share of sorrow in being called on to part with my dearest and lost. 'Tis hard, very hard, to accustom ourselves to such losses, but He directeth all things well and doubtless our dear ones will inherit the Kingdom of the Blessed and have only crossed the silent river a little before us, to intercede for us with our Savior at the bar of a merciful God."

But before these deaths, Eliza had given birth to two other children, Bruce and Alexander Joy III. Born on November 18, 1853, Bruce seemed to have the strong physical constitution of his father, and he outlived him by several decades. On February 26, 1855, Alexander III was born. Both boys eventually married and brought grandchildren into Alick and Eliza's lives, and both joined Alick in his business. But before that, the early lives of both boys would give their parents a good deal of concern. Would they survive the epidemics always breaking out in Hawaii? And would they become honest, upright men? Alick was to be sorely tested.

The small pox epidemic of 1853 and the malaria contagion that swept the islands were a major concern. But, born in Hawaii, both Bruce and Alexander Jr. remained immune to tropical diseases. It was the old missionaries' problem of raising boys in the unsettled culture of Hawaii then sending them to the mainland for education that really caused Alick endless worry. Bruce was always, as Alick once wrote, "a kind, warm hearted boy with heart and hand ever open to the distress of others. God keep him so." After Bruce completed grade and middle schools at Punahou, Alick sent him to a private academy, St. Augustine's Military School, in Benecia, California. Residence in California made it possible for Bruce to return to Honolulu every summer. He spent four years at St. Augustine's and was a member of its first graduating class. His father worried over Bruce continually. He even gave Bruce elaborate advice about numerous small matters, such as the dangers of swimming. And when he heard that Bruce had come down with a serious illness during the term at St. Augustine's, he was in a frenzy. Bruce told him that until the pain became unbearable he had neglected to treat medically a single pustule that in six weeks' time had grown into a disease over his whole body. Finally, he wrote his father about his illness. "Great God," Alick exclaimed, "the disease [was] lurking in his pure blood for *six . . . weeks.*" He begged the military commandant at the school: "will you be a father to my poor suffering boy and have him attended to as if he were your own son? Spend *all that is necessary.*"

Following graduation in 1873, Bruce entered the University of Vermont, where he continued to play baseball as he had done at Punahou. After graduation in 1877, he returned to Honolulu. Between 1877 and 1881 Bruce had his own "wild days." He confessed that during this time he was "prodigal, profligate & wild." By 1881 he began to wish to erase his wild record and reform his life. He made periodic trips to San Francisco. On one of those, in 1881, he followed his father's advice: "Look around for a good wife," Alick had suggested, "but do not be too precipitate." He married Mary ("Mollie") Louise Wells of Oakland, returned with her to Honolulu, took a house in the Nu'uanu Valley (not far from his parents), and soon had two children, Bruce Jr. and Kathleen.

With Alexander Joy Cartwright III it was a different story. He began well, following DeWitt and Bruce in going to the mainland for continued education. Like Bruce, he enrolled in St. Augustine's Military School. Clearly, however, he was more engaged with sports and social activities than with academics. He was a big, attractive man, six foot four and weighing over two hundred pounds, and he loved baseball and a good time in general. He did some heavy drinking and womanizing and borrowed money to support his habits. Alick was well aware that a weak point in Allie's character concerned women, and he understood that Allie would give all the money he had to any woman that he fancied. Obviously, Allie gave little thought to a career in business. In the late 1870s he married a part-native Hawaiian, Teresa Owana Pratt, and had two daughters, Daisy and Eva; still, he had little direction in life. He looked to his father for almost all of his support. In writing to his brother Alfred, Alick gave a candid, objective, and yet loving assessment of Allie's temperament and attitudes:

> He is very democratic in his ideas and of a very kindly disposition, but these lead him into extremes, as he [too easily makes] his acquaintances of the lower classes . . . his chosen friends. He is exceedingly fond of spirits and is a natural born cock-fighter. His love of fowls and animals of all kinds, particularly hound dogs and [cocks] . . . amounts to a passion. He has no idea of the value of money . . . he will borrow and get into debt if he can. I have advised, lectured, preached and threatened.

Predictably, in marriage it was Allie, not Bruce, who was "too precipitate." Teresa became pregnant before they were married, and her step-father, Pratt, threatened to blow Allie's brains out if he refused to marry his step-daughter. Marriage only increased Allie's wild ways. With no settled home and an unhappy marriage, he spent his time hunting and riding, or on anything else that would take him away from his domestic unhappiness. In 1882 Alick became concerned over the dramatic increase in Allie's expenditures. He wrote to his namesake that between 1880 and 1882, he had given him $8,200 with nothing to show for it—only God knew, Alick lamented, how it was spent. In desperation, he sent Allie to California, placing him under Alfred's care, and arranged to have him admitted to Heald's Business College in Oakland.

A more mature Bruce reflected Alick's disapproval in writing sternly to Allie in July of 1882. He rehearsed a history of the Cartwright family for Allie's sake. All the Cartwrights had led productive, respectful lives, he pointed out. Uncle Benjamin had been the chief cashier for forty years at the First National City Bank in New York. Allie's grandfather, the first Alexander Joy Cartwright, had been "a skilled seamen" and a reliable man. (Bruce even referred Allie to Morrill's *Voyages*, where Grandfather was described as a "fine, polished gentleman and as skillful a seaman as ever walked the decks of a ship.") And, finally, Bruce concluded, everyone respects Father as "a thoroughly upright and just man." Now came the culminating question: "Are you the first of our name to fall from this high state?" It was Allie's duty, Bruce argued, to reform his ways, get his marriage in order or dissolved, and become serious about getting an education that would equip him to pursue a business career. Instead, Allie had recently been borrowing even more money and still relied upon Alick to discharge his obligations.

It was "the meanest kind of dishonesty," Alick wrote to his son, "to incur debt where you have no means of further payment or when you rely upon my generosity." In 1882 he finally refused to pay any more of Allie's debts. He lamented: "I am sick of it all, sick in body and mind and I have determined to put a stop to it. Other fathers have had worthless sons and have discarded them. Why should not I?" To pile grief on grief he also learned that Allie had stopped attending classes at the business college. He pleaded with his youngest child: "Be upright and take your place in the balance of your life among good and true men . . . cut all your old disreputable acquaintances."

Bruce urged his brother to follow his own example: "I am painfully aware of my own shortcomings," he told Allie, "that it seems almost like hypocrisy to point out to you the road you should travel to have an honorable and noble life." For himself, he said, "Long ago I made up my mind to become a straightforward and upright man because I felt it my duty to my kind, indulgent father, to my poor sick mother, & to you." He confided in Allie that their father has had "many a sleepless night & sick headaches embittered by your ingratitude and disregard for his wishes." Indeed, Alick himself had written to his brother

Alfred that the experience had been "a sore trial and has affected me more than the loss of my other children."

The root cause of the problem lay with Allie's casual view of life. But like many a doting parent, Alick suspected that in more immediate terms Teresa was the problem. He and Bruce began to make inquiries into her activities, and what they found disturbed them greatly. Certainly, she was responsible for most of the wild spending. When Bruce and Alick used a private detective and looked more deeply they were still more troubled. Alick put it bluntly when he remarked that Teresa "was a bitch of the first water . . . whoring to her heart's content." For Alick it was a "mystery" that Allie could have tolerated Teresa's infidelities for so long, or remain unaware of them. "I am satisfied," Alick wrote, "that she is a thoroughly depraved woman." They found that "she keeps bad company, spends her time on the streets, neglects her appearance, writes letters to hack drivers, etc. etc." Bruce revealed to Allie that Teresa was "in the habit of going to an assignation house. . . . Her name is also coupled with the names of a number of reckless half whites of low character." The detective had also gotten hold of her correspondence with Simon Brown and several other men including "a low Bus driver," and he stated that there could be no doubt of her infidelities. But, Alick kindly concluded, for the sake of the children, if there was to be a divorce it would be better not to expose Teresa to public shame and that Allie should take the blame himself.

Alick and Eliza had multiple distresses. The paramount one was Teresa's evident neglect of her two little girls. They took one child into their care, and the Pratts took the other. Alick also saw to the support of Teresa, sending her fifty dollars a month. But close behind their material concerns were fears about the negative psychological effects on Allie of continuing in a miserable marriage. Evidence soon came to light that he, too, could be charged with adultery. Teresa called upon Eliza and accused Allie of "many things," concluding by stating that she never cared for Allie and that he could live in San Francisco for all she cared. Allie seemed to have been helpless to do anything about the chaos that he and Teresa were fashioning. Alick persuaded him to stay in Oakland and stick it out where he could attend Heald's Business College while awaiting further developments. The separation was meant to place Allie far away not only from Teresa's influence but from his sporting, good-time friends. Alick finally determined that the only hope for Allie's future lay in a divorce, and this was speedily effected early in 1883. By November of that year, Allie was married again, to Florence ("Susie") McDonald of Benecia, California. Alick was overjoyed when he met Susie and wrote to his sister Kate that Allie's new wife was "just as good as she looks, and Eliza and I are delighted with Allie's choice." In fact, to everyone's surprise, Allie now made the turnaround that Alick yearned to see. He and Susie had two daughters. Allie settled down into his marriage, studied bookkeeping, and joined Alick's business, where Bruce was already taking on a great deal of the work. He continued to love a good time and remained especially passionate about baseball, but he became the "upright man," loving father, and solid citizen of his Alick's dreams. So, eventually, despite rough times, Alick saw his hopes realized and reincorporated his company as Cartwright and Sons Co., Ltd.

Business was booming. To add to all his varied commercial ventures, Alick had moved into a new economic area. He was about to become part owner of a sugar plantation.

KING SUGAR

The first sugar plantation in Hawaii was established in 1835 at Koala. Before the development of a plantation there, employment for native Hawaiians was almost entirely restricted to what was called "chief labour," that is, work done for the sake of the chief and for which the earnings went not to the worker but to the chief. After introducing "free labor," the developer of the Koala Plantation regarded his enterprise as not only a business proposition but also, idealistically, as an "entering wedge, a means of freeing Hawaiians from the miserable system that had prevailed." The author of *Pau Hana* describes the "miserable" system of "chief labour" as follows:

> The King owned all the land and chiefs holding land did so for payment of loyal services and dues. The common people or *makaainana* . . . had to labor for the king or local chiefs, [and] the ali'i. Kapus, or tabus, strictly enforced by the *ilamuku*, or police . . . severely restricted their activities and ambitions. Commoners were subjected to hard labor, heavy taxation, and cruelty. If they were lax in performing labor for their chief, they were expelled from the land or were even subject to a death penalty. They held the chiefs in "great dread" and lived in a state of "chronic fear." Theirs was a life of weariness.

The plantation in Koala began to change the old system. Workers were paid one real (or twelve and a half cents) per day and given food and shelter in addition to wages. The result was that the twenty-three natives who began working at Koala in September of 1835 "sprang" to their tasks, and by "sundown [of their first day] finished their stint." Wages were paid by scrip, chits that could be exchanged for goods at the company store, a practice that became the standard for later plantations. At one stroke, the "freed" natives became workers and consumers. The system satisfied the need of the plantation owner for increased numbers of workers, and therefore larger profits, but it also served the native workers. Within three years of its founding, one hundred men, women, and children lived and worked at Koala Plantation.

Native women were employed at Koala and were paid only half the wages of men, though they proved to be better workers. All hands worked from sunrise to sundown, with time off for meals, four days a week. From Friday through Sunday, the workers cultivated their own taro plots and had time for recreation. Freed from the chief system, the natives were plunged into a new world of modern industrial agriculture, involving strange machinery, fixed time schedules, wages, and Caucasian overseers. At Koala first, then at many other plantations, the modern American world was bidding to transform the organization and customs of traditional Hawaiian culture.

Inevitably, a gap opened between the expectations of modernity and tradition. The native Hawaiians had difficulty adjusting to the new organization of life on the plantation. Compared to the newly arrived Chinese immigrants at Waimea, they were soon regarded as inefficient and unruly. The result, easily foreseen, was that as early as 1838, plantation owners began to look to increasing number of immigrants from China to supply new workers. The Chinese eventually drove out the Hawaiians. The globalization of the plantation had begun.

In the first three years of production the Koala plantation shipped 30 tons of sugar and 170 barrels of molasses to Honolulu. Without a doubt sugar was ready to become a new cash crop for Hawaii. By 1846, the *Sandwich Island News* reported that sugar was established as a real and potentially important source of economy for the Islands. By 1848, sugar was beginning to be a fixed component of Hawaii's export trade. A great boost to the development of sugar occurred in 1848, with the "Great Mahele" ("Division"), when the government approved the division of Hawaii's lands, previously entirely owned by the king, among the crown, the government, chiefs, natives, and other settlers. Shortly afterward, private land ownership was extended to foreign residents. Private land ownership inevitably opened Hawaiian enterprises to local planters, land speculators, and even foreign investors. Sugar was on its way to being pronounced "king." By 1849, when Cartwright arrived, many entrepreneurs were beginning to speculate in sugar, for it was clear that cane grew abundantly in the warm Hawaiian climate. Cartwright was perfectly aware of the potential for speculation in sugar, since his first employer, A. B. Howe, began to establish a sugar plantation shortly after Cartwright arrived, during the first years of their relationship. Howe was already talking about his plans in 1849, and on September 27, 1850, he gained a patent on 133 acres of land at Mananalua in Hana on Maui. By 1851 he had negotiated a government loan of $3,000 from Gerrit P. Judd, Hawaii's minister of finance. He purchased equipment, erected buildings, and hired native Hawaiian workers, and in short order he commenced to cultivate sugar cane. Unfortunately, Howe died in November 1852 at the house of Minister Judd. The result was not an uncommon one in a new, developing society. It was alleged at the time that there were financial shenanigans and that Judd himself bought the distressed property at a low price in a government sale, assumed the loan, removed the valuable equipment as well as the matured sugar cane, and then defaulted on the loan. Cartwright, who with the death of Howe had to seek another job, watched with his usual stoicism. He learned two lessons: that considerable profit could be gained in sugar and that it was wise to be cautious in the sugar boom atmosphere of the islands.

If sugar was not yet king by 1852, it was assuredly part of the lesser nobility—and it was being noticed. The New Orleans journal *DeBow's Review*, printed an article in 1857 predicting that the Koala Plantation, "with proper machinery . . . is capable of yielding five hundred" tons of sugar per annum. During the Civil War in the United States the price of sugar rose from four cents a pound in 1861 to twenty-five cents a pound in 1864. No wonder that in the same year the *Commerical Advertiser* of Hawaii predicted that with plantations sprouting up on all the islands, sugar would soon become "the great staple of the islands." Finally, in 1877 the *Hawaiian Gazette* announced confidently: "It is apparent that Sugar is destined most emphatically to be 'King.'"

When the U.S. and Hawaiian governments agreed upon the Reciprocity Treaty in 1875, sugar took another leap forward. One part of the treaty granted Hawaii the right to export sugar to the mainland duty free. This promised huge profits for sugar planters; investors, too, could count on at least a 10 percent dividend. Eventually, dividends on some plantations rose as high as 60 to 100 percent. The press caught on at once and trumpeted the boom: "Thus we hear," the *Pacific Commercial Advertiser* proclaimed in 1877, "of persons, heretofore engaged in multifarious businesses, professional men, clerks, employers—in short, individuals representing all classes of the community—talking of making a venture in cane sugar." Koala had produced 30 tons from

1835 through 1837; by 1878, nearly 30,000 tons of sugar was being exported annually from Hawaii, with a value of about $1,800,000. Initially, Alick had spoken vehemently against the Reciprocity Treaty, believing that it would benefit no one but the planters. He treated the matter ironically in March 1876: "Everyone is waiting for 'Reciprocity,' the magic wand that is to convert our fallow acres into fertile fields, our poverty into riches, the abracadabra, the philosopher's stone, that is to transmute all base metals into the brightened gold. Gold with which we shall be able to pay our debts, national and individual." Later, in October, with some bitterness, he saw the results. "It has helped only the sugar plantations," he wrote, while "taxes were raised on account of that d—d treaty." By this time he had only one hope for Reciprocity—that it would "lead to speedy annexation."

That same year, John Cummins, a prominent businessman in Honolulu, joined with a group of investors to found a sugar plantation in Oahu. Cartwright immediately agreed to invest with Cummins in the venture. If the Reciprocity Treaty favored sugar plantations, well then, Cartwright was now prudently and pragmatically ready to be a sugar planter. By the time that the Reciprocity Treaty was abrogated in 1882, sugar was so established that the duty-free provisions were no longer needed. "Sugar is as much a necessity as tea or butter," Cartwright confidently observed. He was right. Commerce, he told Elias Hempstead, "is dull in everything except the sugar businesses, which through Uncle Sam's good nature, is making the fortunes of Germans, English, Chinese, and a few American planters." Making use of his personally close relation to King Kalakaua, Cartwright helped to arrange for Cummins to lease 7,900 acres of royal land to cultivate sugar cane. By then Cartwright knew the facts of the sugar business inside and out. He had been insuring sugar plantations since the 1850s, and this had become a major part of his insurance agency. In 1878, the other major parts of his insurance business, shipping and investments, were depressed, but sugar was booming and he focused his attention on it. "Money and Exchange are awfully tight and hard to get," he wrote to his old friend John R. Cashman in 1879, "but Sugar's plentiful." No wonder he could tell Joseph B. Berrill that though business and money was "tight," "I have thus far not felt any pressure [personally] and have been able to help quite a number who were short." As always with Cartwright, his increase in funds was rapidly followed by an expansion of his charity.

Two other developments occurred in the late 1870s. Cartwright began to spend almost all of his time at the house that he had built on the property given to him by Queen Emma at Waikiki. Given the longer time needed to commute to downtown, he spent fewer hours at his office than when he had lived only blocks away from the Mahoe Building on Queen Street. Now, he moved his business—Alex J. Cartwright, Esq., Shipping and Financial Agent—to the offices recently vacated by the Bishop & Co. Bank on Kaahumanu Street. He was at his office only from nine to five, five days a week. He would occupy this space for the next ten years.

Cartwright's gamble in sugar paid off. "The sugar (and rice) business is going to pay enormously" he told his brother Alfred. And so it did, making a fortune for Alick. His sugar plantation was located at Waimanalo, on the eastern coast of Oahu, about ten miles from Honolulu. However, the mountain range between Honolulu and Waimanalo made the trek there an arduous one. Otherwise, the location was favorable, since the sugar could be shipped from a nearby port. On May 1, 1878, only fifteen days after the incorporation of the plantation, Cartwright invested $1,000 in the Waimanalo Sugar Company, and he continued to acquire shares until he became a major stockholder. At a meeting of the stockholders on April 30, 1879, Cummins was elected president and Alick, treasurer. Cartwright's influence and business sense led him to advise Cummins on all aspects of the Waimanalo Plantation. Contracts between the planters and the plantation workers, Alick insisted, must be made "upon a just and equitable basis." As to the oversight of the plantation itself, Cummins would be personally responsible, but Cartwright prudently counseled him to "exercise the utmost care and economy for the Mill and for the planters, get all the juice you can out of the cane, and all the sugar you can out of the juice. Do not be niggardly . . . but do exercise wise economy." Only a few months later, Alick returned to similar urgings: "work everything [on the plantation] up to its full capacity, and as economically as possible with a view to getting off as large a crop as possible by the end of the year." He went into great detail, even asserting that a "new boiler" would be "of great service" but wondering, "can we afford it?"

We have a vivid picture of the Waimanalo plantation because Daniel E. Bandmann, a British Shakespearian actor visiting Hawaii, wrote a lively account of a trip to Waimanalo in *An Actor's Tour* (1885). Bandmann arrived in Honolulu on December 23, 1884, and soon after was invited to Waimanalo. He describes his departure for the plantation, "with a thousand expressions of Aloha," from his new friends in Honolulu. To get to Waimanalo he rode on horseback and eventually reached the highest peak in the neighborhood, where a scene opened to view of surpassing beauty, leaving on the mind impressions never to be effaced. . . . Beneath us, in the valley of Waimanalo, we could now see the rich sugar plantation, sugar mills, keanini polisates (village houses), and charming meadow-lands that constitute the estate of John Cummins; while beyond these, spreading far and wide, the ocean, serenely quiet; the blue above, the blue below, smiling at each other.

Bandmann goes on to describe a great dinner there. The king was present, wearing a dark blue suit with a crimson sash, covered with leis. The banquet was sumptuous:

There were meats, poultry and game, vegetables and fruits, served in every conceivable mode; boiled, stewed, roasted, fried, and raw . . . dishes of luau pork, mutton, and beef; fish, chicken and duck; sweet potatoes, prepared in all styles; three different sorts of poi—owena, shua, and apuwai; eike bar-narnarno, in all shapes; ham and eggs; sea-eggs; opihi, wana, kukui nuts; and at least forty or fifty other dishes, served with beer, lemonade, milk, and iced champagne of the best quality; while during the whole repast, the king's singers regaled the guests with melodious native songs, and kept us in pleasant wonder and cheerful astonishment.

Dinner was followed by a performance of the hula-kui, and the festivities continued long into the night. In the morning, the party rode on the plantation's railway to the coast, where they boarded the plantation's steamer for the trip back to Honolulu. Such was the life in the plantation for the owners and their guests.

Bandmann does not mention whether he met Cartwright at the Waimanalo Plantation, but he did have contact with Alick in Honolulu. A few days after returning from his visit to Waimanalo, Bandmann acted the lead in the play *Narcisse* for the benefit of the Honolulu Library and Reading Room Association and received from the directors, including Alex J. Cartwright, a cordial letter of thanks.

Bandmann's account also gives an interesting and relevant perspective on the ethnic makeup of plantation workers. The first workers on the plantations were, of course, native Hawaiians. But plantation managers complained about their diligence as workers. In a rather stereotypical way, Bandmann gives the reason: "The Hawaiian is by nature," he observed, "of a happy and generous disposition. He looks on life as a thing of joy. He has all the instincts of a gentleman and is happy in his idleness." But this admirable disposition was ill suited for work on plantations. Bandmann also points out another important fact: the decreasing numbers of native Hawaiians. In 1853, Hawaiians and part-Hawaiians represented 97.1 of the population, 71,091 of 73,137 inhabitants, while Caucasians represented only 2.2 percent of the population. Bandmann clearly foresaw the eventual dissolution of the native population. "Small-pox and leprosy, introduced by the Chinese," and "excessive drinking amongst the natives" led him to conclude that "if things continue as they are . . . there seems nothing to be looked for, save the total extinction of the Hawaiian race."

In the late 1870s and early 1880s, the sugar plantation owners began to rely more and more on Chinese labor. The ethnicities of the workers who came to Hawaii to labor on the plantations would have an important influence on the further development of baseball in Hawaii during Cartwright's life. By 1880 Cartwright was noting that immigrants of several different ethnicities were now on the way to Honolulu. Class conflict was inevitable, and the Chinese soon learned to organize frequent strikes on the plantations to gain more benefits and improvements in working conditions. The owners and managers responded. Robert Hall, manager of the Niulii Plantation, pinpointed the problem: strikes were effective when plantation workers were united by a common ethnicity. To other plantation managers he proposed a solution, "a judicious mixture" of nationalities to "modify the effect of a strike." The manager of the Makee Sugar Company joined in: "Keep a variety of laborers, that is different nationalities, and thus prevent any concerted effort in case of strikes, for there are few, if any, cases of Japs, Chinese, and Portuguese entering into a strike as a unit." The growing strength of the Chinese workers was also noticed by the Hawaiian government, and in 1883, legislation was passed that restricted Chinese entry to 600 immigrants in any consecutive three-month period. Three years later, the entry of all unskilled Chinese was completely prohibited. The fact that about half of all Chinese immigrants returned to China after accumulating some savings also tended to lower the population of the Chinese workers, keeping it unsettled, somewhat fluid, and less likely to bargain effectively.

In order to minimize collective action, the plantation owners steadily diversified the ethnic mix of their workers. Portuguese from the Azores and Madeira were brought in and proved to be good workers, but they did not arrive in great numbers. By the very early 1880s, or even in the late 1870s, planters began to turn to Japan for mass importation of workers for the rapidly increasing number of plantations. Soon, Japanese workers outnumbered the Chinese. Some measures then had to be taken to limit Japanese bargaining power. In a striking reversal, increased numbers of Chinese workers were recruited.

By the time of the formation of the sugar plantation at Waimanalo, King Sugar had transformed homogenous Hawaiian society and created a society there of multiracial and diverse ethnic cultures. As early as 1852, plantation workers were recruited from China. In the late 1860s, African Americans, former Southern plantation hands, emigrated to the Hawaiian plantations. This continued past 1880; in that year Cartwright remarked to Elias Hempstead that most of the immigrants headed to Honolulu were still Chinese. To prevent ethnic solidarity among workers, plantation owners then turned to Japan, the Philippines, and the Azores and Madeira. The Europeans who arrived from Ireland, Norway, and Germany tended to rise to become *luna*, or foremen, overseers. A bit later, Puerto Ricans and Koreans were brought in. To a large extent, this ethnic variety arose from the commercial rapacity of the planters, but it created a remarkable global society that eventually would precede and foretell twenty-first century globalization. Hawaii prophesied the future.

Baseball would prove crucial to this developing society of ethnic variety. Baseball led to ethnic contact and integration more effectively than any social program could have done.

BASEBALL ON THE PLANTATIONS

E ventually, the varied ethnic groups, with their many different languages and customs, would be brought together by sports competition, and this, as it turned out, meant baseball—teams, leagues, and all-star contests.

To make the arduous life on the plantation bearable, recreation was necessary and inevitable. Leisure habits, of course, reflected each ethnic culture and were invariably practiced within cultural confines. Some individuals fished or went to taxi-dances or visited weekend prostitutes for individual recreation. Small groups gambled with cards or on cockfights. Music and dancing were enjoyed by larger groups but were organized according to national tastes.

But it was baseball, the American national sport, that was destined to bring the various ethnic groups together and cause them to associate with other groups through competition. Two historians write, "Baseball had several advantages over other sports in becoming the dominant sport in Hawaii. Unlike football and basketball a player's physical size was immaterial. In a society of wildly disparate sizes and shapes, baseball was . . . conducted on a level playing field." The powerful Hawaiian Sugar Plantation Association saw the value of baseball, which girls and boys and adults could all play, which spectators could enjoy, which was healthy, fairly inexpensive, and, finally, "American" in spirit. Managers were urged by the HSPA to provide for plantation families "a baseball ground well laid out and grassed." A diamond, the association argued, could be "afforded by every plantation," and it recommended, "to encourage this sport, which every nationality of laborers is keen for, prizes could be offered to winning teams." In contrast to gambling, drinking, and sexual promiscuity, which tended to have negative effects on the workers, baseball would "cultivate a spirit of contentment among the laborers."

Baseball had been adopted by the missionaries at the Punahou school to foster or maintain the American spirit in their upper-class children and to Americanize the native Hawaiians being educated there. In retrospect, it was inevitable that baseball would also be adopted by workers on the plantations. Financial considerations coincided with moral aspirations and with national pride, making baseball an obvious choice. After all, the sort of American missionaries who designed and promoted the program at Punahou and other schools on the islands were just as busy in bringing the word of God and American assumptions to the plantations. Hardly had a plantation opened before a church was also built. For instance, immediately after Chinese workers arrived in sufficient numbers to displace Hawaiians in sugar production, the missionaries followed. They distributed Chinese translations of the Bibles and religious publications to Chinese plantation laborers. In 1867 the Hawaiian Board of Missions made an effort to give a Chinese translation of the New Testament, a "very neat little volume, beautifully printed," to every Chinese worker. The Chinese were not "mere chattels," the association said; rather, they possessed "rational and immortal souls" and had the same "natural rights" as all others.

As each new nationality arrived, the same process was repeated. Soon, not far from the church, a baseball field was laid out—diamond shaped, and precisely on the principles and rules written out by Alexander Joy Cartwright in 1845—and the process of Americanization continued in the islands, focused on working populations that had assembled there from all parts of the world.

Baseball caught on with astonishing speed wherever sugar plantations were established. William R. Castle remembered that "in the late 1860s or early 70s, I rode through the town of Waiohinu [in Kauai]. I passed the town park . . . and was much interested to see a full fledged ball match in progress. All the countryside was on hand, deeply and enthusiastically interested. . . . [I] saw some pretty good ball playing." Baseball developed into a family sport. Girls and boys both played, and men of all ages played nearly every evening since by the 1880s work on the plantations generally ended in the late afternoon. As one writer put it, baseball fostered "personal, family, and community pride" on the plantations. On Saturdays, crowds of hundreds of men, women, and children would watch the games. At first, baseball gave unity to each separate ethnicity. Later, inevitably, the teams of the groups were brought together in competition. At first, the Chinese teams dominated. Chinese baseball even produced two legendary players, Kanky Chun and En Sui Pung, called "the Ty Cobb of Chinese baseball" by Wayne Sakamoto. More than a decade before Reverand Takie Okamura began to organize Japanese baseball through his boarding school, the Chinese on the plantations and, a bit later, in the cities, were playing a remarkably strong game. They were superior in talent to the visiting college teams from Japan and beat them handily. Around the turn of the century, several championship Chinese teams went on the barnstorming tours throughout Asia. In Hawaii, they dominated baseball until the end of World War I. Later, the Japanese fielded the best clubs. Baseball had been developed in Japan itself for several decades by then. The surge of Japanese baseball in Hawaii reflected a new community spirit. Jimmy Wasa, a Moiliili resident, remembered that the community leaders would "scold" the players for "fooling around" on a Saturday night since they "should be at home resting for the game on Sunday. . . . They all felt a common cause. . . . That's why the Plantation encouraged and promoted the game to the workers." But on any particular plantation, ethnic pride ran high, the various nationalities played hard, and victories came to every group.

Without anyone precisely anticipating it, baseball began to provide a common language—"balls" and "strikes" and "bases" and "bats" were just the beginning of a common vocabulary. Teammates of a runner steaming for "home" would call out "slide" and other such recommendations in English, not in their native languages. The process of language learning was further accelerated when teams began to be formed in relation to work duties on the plantation. Field workers, cutters, drivers, mill workers, juice pushers, mechanics, garage workers, *luna*, staff, and managers formed their own teams. When there were a large number of workers in a work duty, as there were in the case of the field hands, more than one team could be organized. Staff and managers could form only one team. Soon, the various levels of workers were arranging rival contests. "Every plantation had several baseball teams," according to the authors of *AJA Baseball in Hawaii*, and these "eventually formed a league" inside each plantation.

The profusion of languages evolved into a common baseball language, which was necessarily English. But one other important effect soon appeared. Workwise, the plantations were rigidly hierarchical, with the managers on top and the field workers at the lowest rung. But in baseball, no class hierarchy could long endure. Talent crossed classes, and as the newest immigrants learned to play the game, they soon began to win against mechanics and even managers.

So passionate about baseball did the workers on the always increasing number of sugar plantations become that rivalry between plantations eventually became possible. From the varieties of workers and ethnicities, multiclass and multiethnic "all-star" teams were gathered to challenge the best players of nearby plantations. An all-star team on a particular plantation might be composed of several different ethnicities—from Chinese or Filipino field workers, say, along with a Portuguese *luna*, and a couple of Scots-American managers, while another plantation might have mostly Japanese hands and former African American slaves, a Spanish overseer, and an English manager as team members. These all-stars mixed together freely on the diamond and were applauded by large crowds in equal measure at the big Saturday and Sunday contests.

In Hawaii, baseball was racially integrated long before the birth of Jackie Robinson on the mainland, and this legacy has endured to contemporary times. As Japanese baseball player and entrepreneur Duane Kurisu eventually put it, "I want [Hawaii] . . . to be like in 'Field of Dreams.' One of the players will say, 'Is this heaven?' And I'll say, 'No, it's Hawaii.' It's a cliché that Hawaii is a melting pot—but now this is a melting pot for baseball." This did not happen all at once, of course, but as soon as the plantation owners laid out baseball fields it was inevitable. If the plantation owners had meant to keep ethnic groups disunited by hiring various races and housing them separately on the plantations, they should not have made ball fields and created "King Baseball," for baseball forged the very multiethnic unity that owners had hoped to keep from developing. Baseball organizations led to contact, unity, and solidarity among workers.

During Cartwright's life, he was involved in promoting baseball in Hawaii at Punahou, where his children were enrolled; among adults in Honolulu; and also on the plantations, especially at Waimanalo. Cartwright had sent his children to the Punahou school from the time of their arrival in 1852 until, later, his improving financial circumstances and their ages allowed him to send them to the mainland for their secondary educations. DeWitt and Mary attended Punahou, as did the children born to him and Eliza in Honolulu, Bruce and Alexander III, from 1864 through 1869. Both made outstanding records on the baseball field. After graduation, both went to the mainland for further schooling, but during their summer vacations they returned to Honolulu and resumed playing baseball on a downtown team composed of Punahou students, faculty, and graduates. This team had chosen the name "Whangdoodles." To be sure, the club members discussed in 1875 whether the name Whangdoodles was "a suitable one for such dignified young gentlemen as themselves," but the name stuck until the 1890s, when it was replaced by "Punahou Athletic Club." Under both names, this team dominated Hawaiian baseball while the Cartwright boys played on it. Until 1875, it preserved a pristine record of never having lost a game.

The minutes of the Whangdoodle Baseball Club for May of 1872 reported that the team "expects the Cartwright brothers to return to ballplaying when they return from school in the U.S." Both boys continued to share their father's passion for the game. In 1873, Allie was named captain of the team. In 1875, he was listed in the Whangdoodle box scores as its second baseman. As late as 1884, Bruce was still playing ball—by then the Whangdoodle Club had spawned a "Married Men's Baseball Club," which he played for. He seems to have retired from play shortly after, but in 1886 he was the official scorer for the team's games. Bruce loved baseball, but with Allie it was a passion. His daughter Mary remembered that even during her childhood and youth, "My father played baseball constantly . . . his fingers were all out of shape. . . . We used to go to baseball games every Sunday . . . he took me before I could talk."

Baseball on the plantations was certainly influenced by the ardor with which the game was played by the Punahou school team and the Whangdoodles. W. R. Castle reported finding Hawaiians in Kau who called baseball "the gift of Punahou" and avidly took to it. On Cummins and Cartwright's Waimanalo Plantation, the Chinese were the first group of workers to take up the game. By 1885, the Japanese began to arrive in great numbers. While few of the farmers emigrating to Hawaii from Japan were likely to have actually played baseball in their homeland, the native Japanese embraced the game as early as 1873 as a means of "moral discipline," and when Japanese emigrants arrived at a Hawaiian plantation to find baseball already established there, they adopted it as a link between Japan and the United States.

Baseball was avidly played in towns, at schools, and on the plantations. In Cartwright's Hawaii, the sounds of bat against ball and cheering crowds were everywhere. Cartwright was recognized as an integral part of the history of baseball in Hawaii. In February 1882, the Honolulu Athletic Association was formed and elected "Mr. Alex. J. Cartwright" a Life Member.

With all this baseball furor—and with the celebrated Spalding ball achieving international fame, the stage was set for the next great event in the history of baseball in Hawaii and Cartwright's involvement in it. News began to arrive in the islands that Spalding's Chicago White Stockings, led by "Cap" Anson, were preparing to make a world tour, and their first stop was to be Honolulu. But best of all, the "celebrated" Spalding himself, the pitcher, All-Star, and great promoter of baseball, was to arrive in Hawaii with the team.

SPALDING'S WORLD TOUR—FIRST STOP, HAWAII

In the late 1860s, the Cincinnati Red Stockings rose to prominence as the premier baseball team in the United States. Harry Wright, formerly a player for Cartwright's New York Knickbockers, had gotten nearly $10,000 from local boosters in Cincinnati to assemble the first avowedly professional baseball team there. Harry's younger brother George starred at shortstop. Against eastern teams the Red Stockings proved to be all but invincible. During 1870, the team won its last twenty-four games. President Grant, himself a well-known baseball enthusiast, welcomed them gloriously when they played in Washington. Between 1869 and 1870, they won eighty-one consecutive games before barely losing to the Brooklyn Atlantics in extra innings. So accustomed were the boosters and the Red Stockings' Cincinnati fans to victory that both abandoned the team with its 81-1 record. With little hesitation, Harry Wright moved his players to Boston. He arrived there with a newly signed star pitcher under a one-year contract, paying him an astronomical $2,500, which made him the highest-paid player in baseball. This man was Albert G. Spalding. The team came together at the same moment that the National Association of Professional Base Ball Players was formed with ten teams. With George Wright in the field and Spalding on the mound, the Red Stockings—later, the Boston Red Sox—won the league championships from 1872 to 1875. Spalding, in particular, dominated the league's hitters with his feared "dewdrop" curveball. In 1875, his final year with the Red Stockings, he had a won-lost record of 55 and 5, with an astonishing earned run average of 1.52, allowing less than two runs a game.

Spalding's greatest talent, as it developed, was not his pitching but his entrepreneurship; he was a born promoter. Chiefly, he promoted himself by signing ever more lucrative contracts. Soon, he jumped ship from the Red Stockings to play in Chicago. There he opened a sporting-goods store, manufactured the new National League's official baseball, and began to publish the league's official yearbook as well as his own annual—*Spalding's Official Baseball Guide*.

Other players had preceded Spalding in capitalizing on their star status in the national sport. In 1874, Harry Wright had taken two teams, his own Red Stockings and the National Association runner-up, the Philadelphia Athletics, on a European tour. Spalding was one of the players, but in his habitual grandiose way he subsequently took credit for the entire tour. "It occurred to me," he later wrote, "that since Base Ball had caught on so greatly in popular favor at home, a couple of teams could be taken over to introduce the American game to European soil." It became Spalding's aim to outdo the previous tour. No wonder that in the late 1880s, with all his other projects flourishing, he began to plan his own world all-star tour, from Chicago to Australia, with a secret plan to continue right on around the world. Play would be between Spalding's Chicago White Stockings, led by the future Hall of Famer Adrian "Cap" Anson, and an all-star team led by another outstanding player, John Montgomery Ward of the New York Giants.

Spalding laid his plans for the trip carefully, intent on not repeating the mistakes that had made Wright's tour a failure and especially on getting maximum publicity both abroad and at home. One of his coups was to arrange an audience at the White House with the current president, Grover Cleveland. The team waited briefly in the East Room while the president installed Melvin W. Fuller as the new chief justice of the Supreme Court. Spruced up for the occasion, the team members looked "as prim as a squad of theological students." Speaking for the group, Anson told Cleveland that the White Stockings sought a "little favor . . . an endorsement" of their tour, bringing the American sport to the world. To further encourage the president, Anson urged: "We are all Democrats, and we will vote for you in November." (If that promise swayed the president, he should have asked Anson to guarantee many more votes, since that fall he lost the election to Benjamin Harrison.) But he did respond favorably to Anson's plea. A few days after the meeting a letter from President Cleveland arrived at Spalding's office, "certifying Anson and his men to be exponents of the great national game of baseball."

They certainly were garbed as representatives of America. John Montgomery Ward's wife, the flamboyant actress Helen Dauvray, designed the uniforms for the All-Stars: cream flannels with a silken America flag encircling the waist.

So attired, the team dueled the White Stockings from Chicago westward across the American continent on the way to Australia.

Their first stop after departure from the mainland on the *Alameda* was to be Hawaii. With no knowledge of how important baseball in Hawaii was, the sportswriter for the *Omaha Herald* called this stop, "BaseBall for Canibals [*sic*]." Scheduled to sail for Honolulu on November 17, the ship waited in port in San Francisco until the next day in order to pick up a large mail shipment from the East Coast, including the results of the presidential election. Their itinerary was thoughtlessly delayed: the teams were supposed to arrive in Honolulu on Saturday, November 24, at six in the morning. A game was scheduled for one p.m. on the very diamond laid out by Cartwright in 1852 at Makiki Field. Its grandstands had been enlarged once again to seat up to 1,800 spectators. Makiki Field's "splendid condition in every way surprised the [mainland] U.S. players," one U.S. reporter wrote. They found the Honolulu diamond "large enough to meet the requirements of the League game. The turf is even and level," and the new grandstand was excellent. A double-header was scheduled; after the regular game between the Chicago and All-Stars teams, the White Stockings were to face "a picked nine from our local [Honolulu] clubs."

But the delay of a day meant that the teams did not sail into Honolulu until five-thirty A.M. on Sunday, November 25. This made "a serious complication," Spalding later admitted. The supposed cannibals of Hawaii turned out to be quite conservative Christians who had scruples against playing baseball on the Lord's Day. The local Punahou A.C. team refused to play on Sundays, terming that "mucker," or lower-class baseball. And besides, the blue laws legislated in Honolulu forbade a game. Nonetheless, Spalding's players were joyously greeted with leis and treated to a sumptuous tropical breakfast at the Royal Hawaiian Hotel, then escorted to the Iolani Palace to meet King David Kalakaua.

There was considerable disappointment in Honolulu at the ship's late arrival, for the local residents were avid baseballers. Discussing the expected arrival of the White Stockings and All-Stars, the "Baseball Giants" and the "Cream of Baseballdom," a local reporter had noted: "There is no community in America or anywhere else which takes a greater interest in base ball than this community; and we confidently expect that the American teams will be received here with whole-hearted cordiality and hospitality." "We found," Spalding later wrote, "that they had four established clubs; that baseball was well under way and fully appreciated." Baseball, he wrote elsewhere, was "solidly established" in Hawaii, which he termed "an American colony in all but name."

Along with Spalding's Hawaiian cousin, George W. Smith, Cartwright had been active on the local committee in making the arrangements for the promised game as well as for the hospitable reception. He was acquainted with Albert Spalding at secondhand, both because he continued to follow news of the development of the game on the mainland and also because he had been an executor of the estates of at least two of Spalding's cousins in Hawaii, and he was intimately acquainted with Spalding's one still-living cousin. We know that Cartwright and Spalding sat down for a chat, since Spalding later recalled in his 1911 book, *America's National Game*, that he found "Cartwright . . . one of the devotees of Base Ball who was deeply disappointed that the boat had not arrived on time and the matches were canceled."

Of course, lacking wireless communication, nobody knew that the ship would be a day late. On the preceding Friday, a Honolulu reporter wrote, "The town is on the tip-toe of expectation. Seldom is the coming of the San Francisco steamer looked forward to with so much unusual interest." Most of the crowd of two thousand that had assembled at the *Alameda*'s dock on Saturday now reassembled on Sunday morning. As the vessel was brought into the slip, the crowd cheered and waved, and the Royal Hawaiian Band struck up "Yankee Doodle" along with the Hawaiian favorite "Aloha-re."

All morning long discussions were held concerning the afternoon's games. Could the king grant a dispensation for play to commence? Could the laws be waived? Might the American Consul, George W. Merrill, settle the question? Certainly, in meeting with the players in the morning at the Iolani Palace, Kalakaua pronounced himself "a fan of the game." "Kalakaua," Lamster writes, "claimed to have played the game himself and his kingdom could boast some baseball royalty of its own: Alexander Cartwright, secretary of the pioneering New York Knickerbockers, had landed in Hawaii as a tourist in 1849 and stayed on permanently."

Spalding knew well that Cartwright had been centrally involved in the origination of the present game of baseball. Perhaps he learned something more about this, too, in talking to Cartwright in Honolulu. In 1904, the year he wrote a speech for delivery at a YMCA Training School event, he stated that members of the Knickerbockers "formulated and published the first rules of the game" in 1845. A year later, in 1905, Spalding cited Cartwright as one of the founders of the Knickerbockers, men who "should be remembered as the founders of our national game." In his 1911 book Spalding himself was much more explicit about Cartwright's role in baseball history. He noted that Alick "was the proposer and prime mover in the formation of the first Base Ball Club . . . the Knickerbockers . . . Club of New York, perfected September 23, 1845, and that he was a player as well as an officer and was an enthusiast to the end." Cartwright, he wrote,

> had a life history contemporaneous with the development of the game he so greatly admired. He had been present when the game was born. He had a part in its first organization. He had witnessed its progress throughout the years of its evolution and had seen it adopted not only as the national pastime of the land of his nativity, but had seen it become the favorite sport of the capital city of that far-off Island of the Pacific which he had adopted as his home.

Here, Spalding all but acknowledged Cartwright as the "maker" or "formulator" of the modern baseball game.

Cartwright himself was ambivalent about whether the promised all-star game should be played. King Kalakaua declared that he would very much like to see the matches. Meanwhile, around the Royal Hawaiian Hotel, where the players were to spend the day, an active petition drive was taking place, and a thousand signatures favoring the staging of the games were collected. A smaller group of signatories raised a purse of $1,000 if the games came off. "I was importuned, almost to tears, to ignore the laws," Spalding recalled. He consulted the city police. The law would be enforced, he was told, and he and his players would be jailed. That settled it. There would be no game. Some of Spalding's party took a carriage out to see Cartwright's Makiki Field. Probably accompanied by Cartwright, Spalding himself went to visit the home of John Cummins.

The players and prominent Honolulu citizens awaited the promised grand treat of the day, a luau on the estate of the Queen. The surroundings were romantic, paradisal—"a perfect fairyland," Spalding's mother remarked—refulgent with tropical fruit trees and royal palms and lighted by Japanese lanterns. Food was piled upon the board in a display of "barbaric plenty." But what the American players found most paradisal of all were the Hawaiian women who greeted them with warm smiles and fragrant leis. "We were all too much astonished . . . to do much else than stare at the dusky beauties as they stood before us," Palmer wrote. To men accustomed to seeing little of the female body in the Victorian United States, these girls, with "their shapely arms exposed—and the brown skin of their rounded shoulders only partly concealed" looked more delicious than any culinary delight. If the descendents of the missionaries had made laws interdicting Sunday baseball, the Hawaiian king had prepared an uninhibited Hawaiian revel. At least this was what the delighted players saw in their fantasies. John Montgomery Ward wrote daringly as a "special correspondent" to the newspaper readers back home:

> All of us knew or thought we knew, that a *luau* was a barbaric festival, fraught with that pagan abandon which obtained in the Sandwich Islands before the day when the good missionaries came and converted the Hawaiians from their wickedness and cannibalism. We knew that these same missionaries had interdicted a game of ball, and we shrewdly suspected that the King, having no sympathy with this inhibition had hit upon the *luau* as a partial reparation to his guests and a bit of revenge upon his Sabbatarian subjects. At any rate, the prospect was delightfully wicked. Besides, whisper it or not, it was vaguely hinted that after the *luau* there would be a *hula-hula*, a dance performed by native girls.

"All day long," Ward continued, the players entertained "visions" of Polynesian girls, "supple of limb and duskily beautiful in every feature."

Ward's guess was very probably correct. The first monarch anywhere to make a round-the-world tour, David Kalakaua was a sophisticated man with a superb command of English, but since his ascendancy to the throne he had been at war with American Victorian customs and culture. Cartwright once remarked that Kalakaua ruled "like an oriental potentate." Even as the upper class of American Hawaiians were intent on stripping him of all but ceremonial power, Kalakaua was intent on restoring indigenous dress, food, and culture, including the dancing of the hula, which had been banned by the missionaries for its sexual suggestiveness.

The Victorians had prevented the playing of baseball on Sunday? Very well, the king would schedule a decidedly anti-Victorian dance on Sunday evening. He arranged for an exhibition of hula. At this "pagan" affront to all decency, Hawaii's attorney general stepped in and put *his* foot down: hula dancing was undesirable; hula dancing on a Sunday was unthinkable. There would be no libidinous swaying on the sabbath. So the king lost this battle.

Or did he? After all, the players' fantasies were realized at the banquet. Concerning the "Kanaka girls," Ward wrote: "Not a sweet creature of them all but

had soulful eyes and small feet. Not one that could resist the ardent smile of a
pale-faced ball-player on deviltry intent. We had been bidden to a purely heathen feast." Plentifully supplied with champagne and beer, if indeed these were
needed, the players found opportunities to wander off into the dim recesses
and byways of the extensive gardens for solitary exhibitions of the hula and
assorted other pleasures. The players were ecstatic. "The lithe forms, graceful
movements, and wondrous eyes of the charming Kanaka dancers will haunt
the boys for many days to come," Ward told the readers of the *Chicago Tribune*. He did not go into details, for he had a wife in New York. Even the somewhat puritanical Cap Anson must have taken a good look too, for he remarked
on the girls' keen, sparkling eyes: "If my boys had them we would lead the batting for years to come." Spalding had claimed that his players were "of clean
habits"—indeed, even "Baseball missionaries"—but many seem to have laid
aside their missionary vocations on this night. As they boarded the *Alameda*
that evening, the happy players paused to offer a rousing three cheers to the
Hawaiians, "especially," Lamster writes, "to the fair maidens." The trip's business manager later reported that at least one of the players had "left his heart"
in Honolulu. As the *Alameda* crossed the coral reef that formed the seawall of
the Honolulu harbor, the electric lights of the city were turned on, and the still
dazzled and ardent ballplayers hung at the rail watching, "long after midnight
[the lights] that were still to be seen twinkling like fire-flies over the water."

Hawaii was the first stop on the round-the-world tour. At its conclusion, on
April 8, 1889, the players and Spalding were feted at a grand dinner in New York
at Delmonico's. Mark Twain gave a speech there that, when printed, was titled
"To a Baseball Team Returning from a World Tour by Way of the Sandwich
Islands." He was mistaken about their route, but he caught the spirit of the
players' experience on their first stop: "And these boys have played baseball
there! . . . [Those] world wanderers who sit before us here have lately looked
upon these things!—and with eyes of flesh, not the unsatisfying vision of the
spirit. I envy them that." Chaucey Depew, powerful chairman of the board of
the New York Central Railroad and later a U.S. senator, went even further than
Twain. He told the 250 guests:

I believe, as I stand here tonight, that all the men who have ever lived and
achieved success in this world had lived in vain if they knew not baseball. . . .
Well, our guests have visited the Sandwich Islands, where, without clothes,
the King and people said, "We understand Christianity, we have eaten the

missionaries—and yet this religion had done us little good, but if this game is a part of Christianity then from this time we are changed men."

For Twain and Depew and, it seems, for most of the players, Hawaii had been the high point of the tour.

For the baseball enthusiasts of Honolulu, the mere fact that Spalding's baseball circus had come to Hawaii gave still further impetus to the development of the sport in the islands. As the writer for the *Hawaiian Almanac and Annual for 1890* put it, that they did not play a game was a "severe disappointment," but "their presence, however, materially strengthened the interest already existing here, so that this year [1889] witnessed an excellent series of league games between five different clubs, for the championship. . . . The American national game has evidently come to stay, and next year will develop still further interest therein."

The game that Cartwright had invented in New York forty years earlier had come to full blossom in Hawaii.

THE FINAL DISSOLVING

Alexander Cartwright and his wife Eliza were fortunate in having strong physical and mental constitutions. Not until he was in his early fifties did Cartwright mention any illness in his extensive correspondence. Indeed, 1873 marks the first year that he complained of being laid up with rheumatism "and all the other ills that flesh is heir to." A little later, he reported to his doctor, Thomas H. Hoborn, that since "taking your medicine I have had no return of my rheumatism." Two weeks earlier he had gone to Kahukua for the healthy climate. He had to be taken on the bed of a wagon ("unable to ride horseback from weakness"), but when he returned the forty miles, he rode on horseback. Still, he was bothered by "an eruption in my face which comes and goes according to the condition of my stomach or liver." For that he was taking a homeopathic medicine prescribed by a Dr. Nichols.

For Eliza's part, Alick wrote in the same year, her "trouble was "chronic diarrhea." "She has no appetite," she "does not eat potatoes, turnips, or any kind of vegetable." Several years later, by 1881, Alick confided to his sister Esther that Eliza also developed "neuralgia, rheumatism, and palpitations of the heart," and until her death she was never free from these ills.

After 1879, Alick's health worsened, for in that year he caught malaria, after going untouched by several earlier epidemics. He told his sister Kate that the illness was "such as I have not had before for 30 years." But he added that he had "every reason to be thankful that I escaped so easily as several young men in the very prime of life died from the effects of the same disease." But for years afterward, he was plagued by "sick headaches" that occasionally left him weak and fatigued.

Despite his maladies, Cartwright continued to manage his business, eventually with the assistance of Alexander III and Bruce, until his death. By the mid-1880s whaling had declined to almost nothing and his commission business had evaporated, but he remained as active as ever in purchasing and leasing land, managing his private bank, and doing fiduciary business involving lending money, discounting paper, and handling foreign agencies; in settling and managing estates in trust; in selling fire, life, and marine insurance; in acting as an attorney; and, of course, in promoting baseball. In 1890, when the Hawaiian Base Ball Association was given a charter by the minister of the interior, the association sold stocks to the public. Alexander Cartwright bought the first five shares.

In the winter of 1891, after a decade of poor health, Alick's brother Alfred died intestate, and Alick was named his executor. In his grief, Alick left Bruce to settle the estate. The assets were sent to Alfred's only surviving child, Mary Murray, living in Oakland.

Alick had not long to live after Alfred. Surrounded by Eliza and Bruce and Allie and their children, at seventy-two years old Alick himself died at his seaside residence at Waikiki on July 12, 1892, just a week before the official close of Alfred's estate. As reported in a native Hawaiian paper, *Ka Leo O Ka Lahui*, the cause of death was "an illness of the throat," most probably throat cancer. His life had been ruled by the simple philosophy that he had summarized years earlier, in 1877, in a letter to Elias Humphrey, a whaling captain out of New London, Connecticut. Humphrey had informed him that a mutual acquaintance had "got religion." Cartwright replied that he was glad to hear of it,

> But to speak the exact truth I have not much faith in . . . sensational religion and I do not believe that religion is a "progressive science." I am a firm believer in Christianity and have the highest respect and veneration for a true Christian gentleman, but I believe that such a character is best proven by one's daily walk in life, by a quiet and unobtrusive character, by unostentatious charity, and by a careful avoidance of all causes of offense against God or man.

The obituaries that appeared in the Honolulu papers on July 13 confirmed that he had lived in the manner that he had described to Humphrey. The *Pacific Commercial Advertiser* devoted two articles to the announcement of his death and the record of his life. "No man in this city was better known here and throughout the Kingdom than the deceased," the paper's editor began,

> and no one was looked up to with greater respect for those sterling quali-
> ties which go to make a kind husband and father, a valuable and useful citi-
> zen and an upright and successful businessman than ALEXANDER J. CART-
> WRIGHT. Many a one can recall assistance financially, or by advice more
> valuable than money, that has served to make him a friend indeed, and his
> death will be felt and his presence missed in a much larger sphere than his
> family circle.

In the *Pacific Commercial Advertiser*'s obituary paper, Cartwright's varied public career was duly outlined, but he was especially lauded for being "a man of erudition, a pleasing conversationalist, and a forcible reasoner." The tone of the obituary indicates that the writer knew him well. He noted that Cartwright "takes a deep interest in history, in science, and in social, religious and other problems. He is thoroughly informed on the political affairs of the entire world, and possesses a brilliant mind and retentive memory."

Alexander J. Cartwright was buried under a pink granite tombstone in what was then called the Oahu Cemetery, on the ewa (or west) side of Nu'uanu Avenue. Eliza survived him by a year and a half, dying on October 9, 1893, and then was interred beside him. In contrast to Alfred, Alick had made a will. Cecil Brown, Cartwright's attorney, prefaced the will in his own hand, describing the conditions under which it was made:

> Mr. Cartwright sent for me . . . he said he wanted [to] make a new will . . .
> on Sunday morning I rec'd a telephone message . . . that business matters
> should be attended to. I went to Mr. Cartwright & had another talk[,] went
> home and drafted a will. Took same & read it to him. He approved of the
> same, & asked myself, Mrs. Bruce Cartwright & the doctor if it was just. We
> told him it was. He signed his name by holding a book and writing on it[,] he
> signed in my presence & Dr. Miner & myself signed in his presence & at his
> request I had the same in my possession until filed in Court—

To this note, Dr. Miner appended a statement that he had attended Alick, wit-
nessed the signing of the will and later saw his dead body. "He was mentally sound. His mind was remarkably clear, he had been suffering from a carbuncle.

The will [was] executed on Sunday & he died on Tuesday." Accordingly, the will was filed on July 18 and went to probate on August 8, 1892, with Bruce and Allie as executors.

Statements by the petitioners and the content of the will itself show that at his death Alexander Joy Cartwright Jr. possessed considerable assets, as follows:

Real estate at purchased prices or tax valuations	$37,495.00
Corporation stocks, at fair value	$29, 825.00
Notes and mortgages, freehold securities	$49, 166.50
Bills receivable and sundry notes of hand, unsecured or secured by endorsements or collaterals	$76, 384.12
Personal property of every description	$5000.00
Cash in Bishop & Co. Bank	$20, 481.30
Total	$218, 351.92

Notice of the upcoming probate having been published in the *Hawaiian Gazette* for three consecutive weeks, the will was probated before the Honorable A. Francis Judd, chief justice of the Supreme Court of the Hawaiian Islands.

The beneficiaries of the will were Bruce and Allie, with the stipulation that during the life of Eliza Cartwright they would pay to her one-third of the income thereof for her sole and separate use, then after her death, to share and share alike.

Reduced to the cold numbers of probate, the life and career of Alexander Cartwright was very successful. But beyond the numbers, he not only invented baseball but possessed a character and led a life on the highest plane of public integrity and inner excellence.

FIGURE 1 (*top*) Members of the newly organized Knickerbockers Baseball Club in their new uniforms, 1845. Alexander Joy Cartwright Jr. is in the center of the back row. To his right is his younger brother Alfred de Forest Cartwright, with his arm draped around Alick's shoulder. *Source*: National Baseball Hall of Fame Library, Cooperstown, N.Y.

FIGURE 2 (*bottom*) *The American National Game of Base Ball*. Lithograph by Currier and Ives showing "grand match for the championship at the Elysian Fields," Hoboken, N.J., c. 1865. *Source*: National Baseball Hall of Fame Library, Cooperstown, N.Y.

FIGURE 3 A. J. Cartwright in San Francisco, 1849, upon completion of his journey across the country. *Source*: Transcendental Graphics.

FIGURE 4 A. J. Cartwright, San Francisco, 1851. *Source*: H. L. Chase, Bishop Museum.

FIGURE 5 A. J. Cartwright, chief engineer, Honolulu Fire Department, 1859. *Source*: Hawaii State Archives.

FIGURE 6 A. J. Cartwright, c. 1861. *Source*: Taber, Transcendental Graphics, Hawaii State Archives.

FIGURE 7 R. DeWitt Cartwright, c. 1863. *Source*: Hawaii State Archives.

FIGURE 8 A newspaper drawing of Mary Groesbeck Cartwright on horseback attending a flag raising by U.S. sailors for a Fourth of July celebration, 1863. *Source*: Hawaii State Archives.

FIGURE 9   Alexander J. Cartwright III, 1876. *Source*: Chas. Lainer, Bishop Museum.

FIGURE 10 Mrs. A. J. Cartwright, c. 1880. *Source*: Theo S. Marceau, Hawaii State Archives.

FIGURE 11 Bruce Cartwright, 1883. *Source*: J. Williams, Bishop Museum.

Opposite page:

FIGURE 12 Monument to Alexander J. Cartwright, Honolulu. This monument has been decorated by visiting baseball luminaries, such as Babe Ruth, who placed leis (Hawaii's flower garlands) on it in the 1930s. *Source*: J. Y. Bowman, National Baseball Hall of Fame Library, Cooperstown, N.Y.

FIGURE 13 Dedication of plaque in honor of Cartwright at City Hall in Honolulu, 1939. "Let's drink to the memory of Alexander Joy Cartwright Jr.!" said Chairman A. L. Castle of Honolulu's Baseball Centennial Committee, following the unveiling of a plaque in Honolulu's City Hall on August 26, 1939, honoring the "Father of Modern Baseball," an early Hawaiian resident. Raising glasses of Hawaii's own pineapple juice in response to the toast are (left to right) Bruce Cartwright Jr., great-grandson of Alexander Joy Cartwright Jr.; Mayor David Y. K. Akana of Honolulu; Castle; and vice chairman A. Lewis Jr. *Source*: N. W. Ayer and Son, National Baseball Hall of Fame Library, Cooperstown, N.Y.

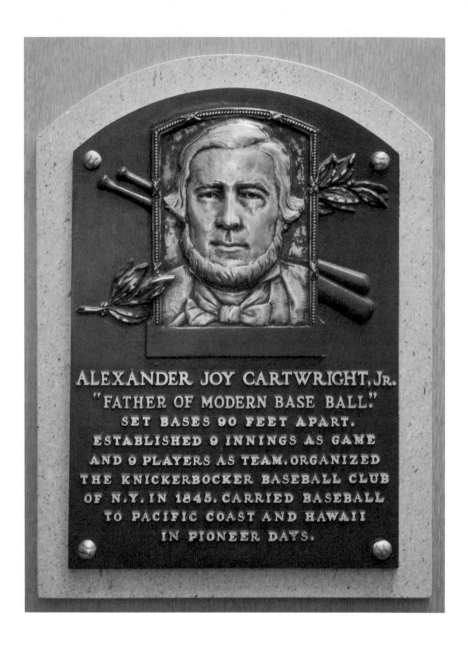

FIGURE 14 Alexander Joy Cartwright Jr.'s plaque at the National Baseball Hall of Fame. Cartwright was elected to the Hall of Fame in 1938. *Source*: National Baseball Hall of Fame Library, Cooperstown, N.Y.

CARTWRIGHT'S SECOND LIFE: MYTH INTO HISTORY

·····································

B oth before and after 1888, Albert Spalding continued to promote baseball—
and himself. By the turn of the century, with baseball firmly established as
the national pastime, the question arose of how baseball originated. Two
schools of thought dominated the debate. The "historicists," as they might
be called, argued that the game evolved from traditional games, especially
English ones, and particularly from rounders, town-ball, or base-ball. The
greatest sports writer of the day, Henry Chadwick, argued for such a historical evolution. On the other side, the "American exceptionalists" argued that
baseball was a uniquely American game. Albert G. Spalding and John Montgomery Ward vigorously represented the Americanist position. Of course,
Spalding and Ward acknowledged that ball games had been played in the
remotest antiquity. Spalding traced them back to Egypt, and Ward went
back to the Greeks, citing the ball game played by Nausikaa in *The Odys-
sey*. But both argued that baseball was uniquely American. "I have never had
any doubt myself that Base Ball was a purely American game," Ward wrote
to Spalding. Spalding outlined his theory to N. E. Young on November 30,
1904: "I believe [baseball] is an entirely American game in origin and came
down from an old Colonial game of 'One old Cat,' which developed into Town
Ball, and then into Base Ball in 1842, the Knickerbockers Club of New York,
organized in 1845, being the first club that I can find any record of." To be
sure, today we are likely to recognize that Chadwick and Spalding were both
right: baseball did develop from a conglomeration of earlier ball games. But
it also took a leap forward from them— in speed, in tightness, and in ritual—
and developed in a uniquely American way with the help of Alexander Joy
Cartwright Jr.

Along with the question of whether baseball was a distinctly American game there naturally arose the question of what individual or group first made a codification of the rules of play that roughly resembled the manner in which baseball was currently played. Besides Cartwright, two players for the Knickerbockers Base Ball Club seemed to be involved. Daniel Lucius Adams, M.D., claimed to be the person who in 1857 set the distance between bases at ninety feet, slightly more precisely than Cartwright's "thirty paces," and to have promoted and solidified the position of the "short-stop." In an interview in 1888 a reporter for the *San Francisco Examiner* interviewed William Rufus Wheaton in Oakland. He spoke of playing for "the Gotham Club" as early as 1837, and claimed that this team abolished "the rule of throwing the ball at the runner." He also claimed that it was he who reduced the rules of the game to writing. But Wheaton's memory seems faulty since William Wood, writing in 1867, asserted that the Gothams always played "the old-fashioned way" of plugging the runners and that no Gotham rule book existed.

In a 1905 editorial Spalding proposed that a commission be established to settle the question. Obviously, Spalding then took a hand in organizing a commission that would be likely to reflect his own views. He saw to it that Abraham G. Mills was appointed chair of the inquiry. Mills had been the third president of the National League. He was called the "Bismarck of Baseball." His intimate association with Spalding is confirmed by the fact that he had been the prime mover and organizer of the splendiferous banquet for Spalding and the players at the conclusion of the round-the-world tour. In addition, Mills, as it turned out, was a crony of Abner Doubleday, a Union general during the Civil War who had been born in Cooperstown, New York. Other committee members partial to Spalding included James Sullivan, the president of Spalding's American Sports Publishing Company; Al Reach and George Wright, who had founded sports equipment companies that were now partially owned by Spalding; and Morgan Buckley and A. P. Gorman, two U.S. senators, who had nationalistic motives for supporting the theory that baseball was distinctly American in origin. Both had attended the homecoming banquet for the team at Delmonico's and were close friends of Spalding. Finally, Spalding found a witness named Albert Graves, "a reputable gentleman," who had lived in Cooperstown, New York, in the 1830s and 1840s. This gentleman asserted with absolute certainty that baseball was an "American game," and that it was invented at Otsego Academy and Green's Select School in upstate New York by Abner Doubleday of Cooperstown. Graves confidently reported:

The American game of baseball was invented by Abner Doubleday of Cooperstown, N.Y., either the Spring prior to or following the "Log Cabin and Hard Cider" campaign of General William H. Harrison for the presidency [i.e., 1840 or 1841]. . . . Doubleday called the game "Base Ball" for there were four bases to it.

Graves's account was prompted by news of the Mills Commission. From Colorado Graves sent his letter to the Akron, Ohio, *Beacon-Journal*, where it was published on April 3, 1905. James Sullivan soon learned of it and brought it to Spalding's attention. The great promoter was so overwhelmed by Graves's statement that baseball was originated by a definite man, in a definite place, at an all but definite time, and with a definite name that he pushed aside all that he demonstrably knew about Cartwright's primary role in baseball's invention. At first he wrote cautiously to Graves to investigate. He admitted to the mining engineer that he was "trying to prove that Base Ball was not of English origin but entirely of American origin." Then he asked basic questions: "Who was Abner Doubleday?" "About how old was he when the incident occurred?" and "Can you positively name the year in which the incident happened?" Graves reasserted what he had already written. Spalding threw caution to the winds, since Graves's account so perfectly affirmed his position against Chadwick's. Your letter, he replied to Graves, proves that "Doubleday was undoubtedly the first starter of Base Ball and quickly superceded Town Ball. . . . It really was an improvement or evolution of Town Ball, and if this is so it directly confirms the contention that I have made." By August, Spalding's excitement ran still higher. He wrote to a Mr. Pratt: "Note what Albert Graves says of a Genrl. Doubleday. . . . From this it would seem that Doubleday was the real father of 'Base Ball' and Cooperstown, N.Y. its birth-place, [and also] . . . Doubleday gave baseball its name."

Soon, Spalding relayed his historic discovery to the Mills Commission and urged its members to issue a report certifying Doubleday's primacy. The report continued the myth making by reporting that Doubleday's plan, "showing the ball field laid out substantially as it is today was brought from Cooperstown to Cartwright's [Elysian] field" by a Mr. Wadsworth, possibly Louis F. Wadsworth, who played first base for the Gothams and Knickerbockers between 1850 and 1852 and was a member of the Knickerbockers as late as 1857. In this narrative, Cartwright was merely the beneficiary of a game invented by Doubleday. But this was at least five years after Cartwright had innovated the diamond and about the time he laid out Makiki Field in Honolulu. What is more, an informant to the investigators later told Mills that upon reflection he had definitely erred in speaking of a "Mr. Wadsworth." He now asserted that the Knickerbocker player Duncan Curry was the man he meant and that Curry had told him that Cartwright, not Doubleday, was the originator of the modern rules of baseball and the design of the field. So, in the end, as Szmanski and Zimbalist write, it was "Cartwright [who] . . . supplied the first unifying basis for the game that previously had been played under different rules in each community." Mills himself wrote in the first sentence of the final report of 1907 that he was originally convinced that "our national game of Baseball originated with the Knickerbocker Club organized in New York in 1845" and that the evidence for Doubleday's origination was "circumstantial." But Graves's "evidence," as reported by the excited Spalding, convinced him that Doubleday had the earlier claims. Mills soon declared that "patriotism and research" had established that baseball was uniquely American and that Doubleday had created it.

The work of the commission had taken three years, and the eagerly awaited conclusion was widely reported in the nation's papers. Baseball was invented by Doubleday, period. The report stuck in the popular imagination. In 1937, during the preparations for baseball's centennial, a New York state legislative committee cemented the myth that Cooperstown was the birthplace of baseball. This promised to be excellent publicity for the promotion of tourism in economically distressed upstate New York, and $10,000 was appropriated to advertise and publicize New York's "historic site." President Franklin Delano Roosevelt of New York was induced to assist the business of the Empire State. He issued a proclamation that read: "We should all be grateful to Abner Doubleday. Little did he . . . realize the boon [he and the other players] . . . were giving the nation in devising baseball." As recently as 1990, New York offered automobile licenses proclaiming New York "The Birth Place of Baseball."

Baseball historians have been more than skeptical. Doubleday was undoubtedly a distinguished soldier and American. But he was a cadet at West Point when he was supposed to be creating baseball in Cooperstown. It appears that he never saw a baseball game, he never played baseball, and certainly he never once mentioned baseball in his numerous printed writings or reported conversations. Robert Smith, author of *Baseball*, put it bluntly in 1948 in a *New York Times* article: "Doubleday never played the game, watched the game or talked about the game." Another sports writer was even more blunt. Doubleday, he wrote, "didn't know a baseball from a kumquat." But for a long time the fable that Doubleday was baseball's inventor was cemented in the popular imagination. In his own publication, Spalding promoted Doubleday, attacked the Knickerbockers as elite banqueters who only played a game among themselves occasionally, and denied Cartwright's contribution.

Spalding's myth became history, at least for a time. But pesky and persistent evidence always suggested that another man had been responsible for codifying the rules and the dimensions of baseball, notwithstanding that the Baseball Hall of Fame was eventually built in Cooperstown, New York, because that was Doubleday's home town and where he was alleged to have created baseball.

Doubleday has never been elected to the Hall of Fame, however. Rather soon, focus tended to fall upon Alexander Joy Cartwright Jr. Many people began to believe what *The Minneapolis Review of Baseball* would succinctly say: "Cartwright invented baseball. Spalding invented Abner Doubleday." An all-star baseball team visited Cartwright's grave in homage to the creator of baseball in the winter of 1923. When the major leaguers arrived back in San Francisco, they told a reporter, "they paid a graceful compliment to the memory of Alexander Joy Cartwright, hailed as 'the father of baseball,' during their brief stopover in Honolulu." In Nu'uanu Cemetery, Herbie Hunter placed a wreath on the tomb. Among others, Emil "Irish" Meusel of the New York Giants, Waite Hoyt, star pitcher for the Yankees, and Amos Strunk of the Chicago White Sox attended, along with local dignitaries Sanford B. Dole and Bruce Cartwright and his family. By the late 1930s, as the presumed centennial celebrations of the invention of baseball approached, doubts concerning Doubleday and questions about baseball's innovator were very much in the air.

On November 4, 1937, Bruce Cartwright Jr. wrote to the centennial organizers to make the case that his grandfather, not General Doubleday, deserved to be recognized for his central and crucial contribution to the formation of baseball as it was still played. Bruce Jr.'s facts and the accompanying documents convinced the committee that Cartwright's claims were valid. In 1938, along with Henry Chadwick, Cartwright was elected to the Baseball Hall of Fame as "The Father of Modern Baseball." In the winter of 1939, when Babe Ruth arrived in Honolulu with his all-star team to play exhibition games, he made the pilgrimage to Nu'uanu Cemetery, where he was photographed placing leis on Cartwright's grave. The Babe declared himself for Cartwright.

That same year a bronze plaque commemorating Cartwright's place in baseball history was installed in Cooperstown, then another at Hoboken at the site of Elysian Fields, and a replica plaque was unveiled at Honolulu Stadium.

August 26, 1939, was declared "Cartwright Day" by Honolulu Mayor Charles Spencer Crane, and the rest of the United States followed. Hawaiian flowers were flown to every city mayor and team manager of a major-league baseball town in the country. At Ebbets Field in Brooklyn, before a crowd of 34,000, the Reds and Dodgers paused before the game to drink a toast of pineapple juice to Cartwright. The drink was served by "Hawaiian maids in grass skirts and bare feet"; they hung a lei around the neck of each player. On the next day, another plaque in Cartwright's honor was placed in the Honolulu City Hall. A street in Waikiki near the location of his residence was renamed Cartwright Street. And Makiki Park, where Cartwright had paced off the oldest, longest lasting modern baseball field in the world, was rechristened "Cartwright Field." The *Honolulu Advertiser* declared unequivocally of Cartwright: "His right to the title, 'The Father of Baseball,' is unquestioned."

The Doubleday myth was dissolving, and the historical Cartwright was emerging. Elysian Fields, the site of the "first recorded match game" soon came in for its share of fame by association with Cartwright. Of course, Elysian Fields had not retained its earlier pastoral splendor. The field that Cartwright had laid out there was paved over to provide parking for the Maxwell House coffee plant that had been built on the spot where the Knickerbockers once played. But at the nearby Stevens Institute of Technology an annual celebration was held, reenacting the 1846 game, with period uniforms and Cartwright's rules, along with modern "Little League games, fireworks, and batting cages, . . . even a baseball card show." Hoboken, the site of Elysian Fields, would call itself "The Birth Place of Baseball." The city fathers even commissioned a country-western song titled "Baseball Was Born in This Town" by Jim Reardon of Asbury Park, and presented the key to the city to Alexander J. Cartwright IV, Alick's great-great-grandson.

In 1955, when a plaque of Cartwright was unveiled in Hoboken, Walter Alston, manager of the Dodgers, attended the ceremony and quipped: "It's a real pleasure to be here and to see such great enthusiasm for baseball. They tell me that Alexander Joy Cartwright, Jr., was an outfielder, infielder, and catcher. I wish he was playing today—we sure could use him."

Many years after Cartwright had set forth the rules for modern baseball and led his team in playing the first recorded games, Cartwright emerged back into history. Decades after his death he still lives in his creation.

CHRONOLOGY OF THE LIFE OF
ALEXANDER JOY CARTWRIGHT JR.

In view of the fact that several sections of this narrative are organized themat-
ically, I have placed this chronology here to guide the reader in a year-by-year
account of Cartwright's life.

April 17, 1820. Alexander Joy Cartwright Jr. is born in Manhattan, second son
of seven children born to Alexander Joy Cartwright Sr. and Ester Rebecca
Burlock Cartwright.

Winter–spring 1837. AJC leaves school and takes a job as clerk in the stock bro-
kerage firm of Coit and Cochrane.

Summer 1840. AJC accepts job as a teller in Union Bank on Wall Street.

June 1842. AJC is married to Eliza Van Wie in the Third Free Presbyterian
Church in Manhattan on Thompson and Houston Streets.

Early 1840s. AJC joins Knickerbocker Fire Engine Co. no. 12. The fire companies begin to organize teams to play baseball.

May 3, 1843. AJC's and Eliza's first child is born, named DeWitt Robinson
Cartwright.

June 1, 1845. A second child, named Mary Groesbeck Cartwright, is born.

September 13, 1845. The "Knickerbockers Base Ball Club" organized by AJC
and six other players.

1845. The Union Bank Building is burned down in a Wall Street fire; AJC is out
of a job.

Fall 1845. With his brother, Alfred de Forest Cartwright, and Henderson Green,
AJC opens a stationery and book store on 67 Wall Street.

Mid-September 1845. AJC codifies the rules for baseball as played by the Knickerbocker team. These became widely adopted as the basis for play in competitions between Knickerbocker players and in games between the Knickerbockers and other teams. AJC also draws up Knickerbocker Club by-laws and designs a mode of scoring games.

October 6, 1845. First game played under what turn out to be the basic rules of modern baseball, at Elysian Fields, near Hoboken, New Jersey. The score is 11 to 8. The Knickerbocker players continue to play intrasquad games through October 18, 1845.

October 21, 1845. Knickerbocker Club challenged by a team from Brooklyn. Knickerbockers win 24 to 4. A rematch is played on October 24.

April 10, 1846. Second season begins.

June 19, 1846. The "1st match game" is played between Knickerbockers and the New York Nine. The New York Nine wins 23 to 1.

1845–1849. AJC records 121 games played by the Knickerbockers.

1848. Gold discovered in California.

March 1, 1849. AJC strikes out for the goldfields of California by the overland route.

July 4, 1849. AJC arrives in Grass Valley and Fort Sutter.

August 10, 1849. AJC arrives in San Francisco. With other Knickerbocker teammates there he introduces baseball on the West Coast.

August 15, 1849. AJC sails for Honolulu, Sandwich Islands.

August 24, 1849. AJC arrives in Honolulu.

October 5, 1849. AJC and Eliza's third child, Catherine Lee Cartwright, is born in New York City.

February 1, 1850. AJC becomes partner in firm of Bowlin and Cartwright, in Lahaina, Maui.

May 1850. AJC returns to San Francisco on a business venture. He makes two more trips from Honolulu to San Francisco in 1850 and 1851.

February 3, 1851. AJC commissioned fire chief of Honolulu; continues until June 1859. Returns temporarily from July 1, 1862, to June 30, 1863.

May 1851. Eliza and three Cartwright children depart for Honolulu.

Fall 1851. AJC helps found Masonic Hawaiian Lodge, U.D., in Honolulu.

November 16, 1851. AJC's third child, Catherine Lee, dies in transit aboard the *Eliza Warrick.*

December 1, 1851. AJC's wife and two surviving children arrive in Honolulu.

April 1852. Bowlin and Cartwright Co. files for bankruptcy.

Spring 1852. AJC lays out a baseball field at Makiki Park, now Cartwright Park, which is still in use after 160 years.

November 16, 1853. Bruce Cartwright is born to AJC and Eliza.

Late 1853. AJC begins business as insurance agent. Buys house in Fort Street in Honolulu.

February 26, 1855. Alexander Joy Cartwright III born.

1855. AJC becomes sales agent to supply a group of whalers from Long Island, New York.

August 1, 1856. AJC leaves Coady & Co.

1856–1892. Charitable and community works.

1862. AJC becomes trustee in administration of estates, as well as land agent and real estate advisor.

1865. AJC becomes acting (later, permanent) consul to Hawaiian Kingdom for Peru.

1866. AJC becomes acting (later, permanent) consul for Chile

June 4, 1869. Mary Groesbeck Cartwright dies in Honolulu.

March 20, 1870. DeWitt Robinson Cartwright dies in Honolulu.

1874. AJC is "Attorney in Fact," to Queen Emma, managing her estates.

1878. AJC becomes partner with John Cummins in the Waimanalo Sugar Company.

February 1882. AJC elected a "Life Member" of the Honolulu Athletic Associates for the encouragement he gave to the development of baseball in Hawaii.

July 12, 1892. AJC dies in Honolulu.

October 9, 1893. Eliza Cartwright dies in Honolulu

1938. AJC inducted into the Baseball Hall of Fame in Cooperstown, New York, as the "Father of Modern Baseball."

DID CARTWRIGHT "REALLY INVENT" BASEBALL? OR, HOW DID THE GAME EVOLVE BEFORE HE ARRIVED?

A Short Survey of Two Vexed Questions

Baseball "fans" are by definition fanatics. Baseball scholars are even more passionate, and, as in their favorite game, choose up sides and proceed to debate endlessly the question first raised by Albert G. Spalding concerning who "invented" baseball. The indefinite nature of the question means an endless number of answers are possible.

My biography of Alexander Joy Cartwright Jr. is not the place to argue protractedly about the many origins of baseball. I take up the subject here, briefly. In recent years several distinguished scholars have minutely examined the complex, multidimensional, evolutionary streams that eventually flowed together to consolidate the game as we know it today. Even now, though, baseball is still evolving. Was the "father" of baseball the first human being to throw a ball at another? Was he (or she) some anonymous figure who caused others to play the primitive forms of games eventually known as "rounders," "base-ball," or "town-ball"? Was he someone who first thought of playing a ball game on a diamond-shaped field? Such distinguished scholars as John Thorn, in books and numerous articles; David Block in *Baseball Before We Knew It*; and Peter Morris in his two-volume *Game of Inches* have exhibited how numerous were the varied threads that wove together from many individual games into a game broadly resembling the one we still play. Like all great social, political, or spiritual movements, all monumental scientific advances, or all inventions, baseball as we know it was "fathered" by an evolutionary process. After all, children and young men had been playing ball as long as anyone could remember. Before any white settlers arrived in North America, the native Indians played several kinds of ball games, mostly involving throwing and catching. Hardly had the Pilgrims settled at Plymouth when, in 1621, the nonseparatists who were mixed into their company ignited the ire of the dissenters by making merry and playing ball on Christmas. Governor William Bradford, ordinarily a man of tolerance, was scandalized to see some settlers "in the streets at play ... at stoole ball." In seventeenth-century America, ball playing of any kind was frowned upon by Puritans. One minister in Kent, Thomas Wilson, was scandalized by observing "Morris-dancing, cudgel-playing, baseball and crickets" played on the Sabbath. But settlers continued to play ball.

On Manhattan Island, where baseball as we know it eventually developed, ball games had a long period of gestation toward the eventual national sport. The Dutch played several kinds of ball, not just the wonderful bowling immortalized in Washington Irving's "Rip Van Winkle" but also games in which balls were thrown and caught and sometimes even struck with a stick. More tolerant than Bradford, Dutch colonists in Manhattan forbade playing ball only during the time when good burghers were expected to be at church. French Huguenots brought their own version of town-ball, called *tcheque*, with them. Even in the late nineteenth century, when Albert G. Spalding's "all-stars" played baseball in Paris, a journalist wrote in *Le Temps* that the game was quite familiar to the French: "Base ball or '*balle aux bases*' is nothing more than a version of the French game *grand thèque* ... which the English call *rounders*." The German immigrants to New York City put their native version of *Ballspiel* into the varied mix. Scots and Irish came, bringing their own sports to mingle with and influence the ball games of the Dutch and French and German settlers. We know from military diaries of the Revolutionary War that ball games were played by both sides—British, Germans, and "Americans"—during long lulls between battles. Our earliest president to play ball was George Washington. George Ewing, a soldier at Valley Forge, wrote in a letter of May 4, 1778, "This day His Excellency [George Washington] dined with G[eneral] K[nox] and after dinner did us the honor to play Wicket with us." Every European who subsequently arrived on American shores knew his own national ball games. New York City was the most cosmopolitan spot for an international amalgam of ball playing. The city was then, and still remains, a fertile ground for ball games. "American" versions of old European ball games were shaped there by varied influences.

The English called one of their ball games "rounders." During the eighteenth century, they also played a game called "base-ball," in which girls as well as boys participated. Americans played "base-ball," too. The earliest mention of the game in New England after the revolution occurred on September 5, 1791, when an ordinance was passed proclaiming that "for the preservation of the windows in the new Meeting House . . . no Person or Inhabitant shall be permitted to play at any game called Wicket, Cricket, Base ball . . . or any other Game . . . within the distance of eighty yards from said Meeting House." Baseball still met with disapproval from religious-minded citizens, and sometimes even intellectuals. Thomas Jefferson wrote in 1795 that "Games played with the ball stamp no character in the mind." Despite such doubters, in eighteenth-century America, base-ball caught on as Puritanism waned; base-ball became so established that a child's primer of 1744 chose the game to represent the second letter of the alphabet.

BASE-BALL

The Ball once struck off,
Away flies the *Boy*
To the next destined Post,
And then home with Joy.

On November 18, 1748, Mary Lipell, Lady Hervey, described what the family of Frederick, Prince of Wales, was doing on that day: "diverting themselves with base ball, a play [with which] all who are . . . schoolboys are well acquainted." Nearly fifty years later, in *Northanger Abbey* (1798) Jane Austen introduced the Morland family in this way: "Mrs. Morland was a very good woman . . . but her time was so much occupied that her elder daughters were inevitably left to shift for themselves; and it was not very wonderful that [fourteen year old] Catherine should prefer cricket . . . [and] base-ball to books." (Since Austen's depiction of Catherine's girlhood is based on her own experiences, it is reasonable to call her the first major author who we are certain enjoyed playing baseball.) America reflected England. Horatio Smith, the English author of *Festivals, Games, and Amusements* (1831) was aware that in "New England . . . the young men are expert in a variety of games of ball—such as cricket, base, cat, football, trapball," and others that were well known in England.

With so many ball games, the rules for each contest had to be negotiated before each game. At what distance were the stakes, stones, or bases to be from one another? How was the field to be laid out? How many players were to constitute a team? What sort of ball was to be used? What made a "run" or a "score"? What constituted an "out"? How was victory decided? Such negotiations might reach easy social agreement in the eighteenth and early nineteenth century in America. Players could meet and settle on the set of rules that accommodated the number and enthusiasms of those gathered. Ball games were played on various sorts of fields and in many different settings. The most common was a vacant field. The village green was often used. Of course, base-ball games were also easily arranged on the quads at eastern colleges, since there was always a sufficient number of potential players in the dorms. Base-ball was verifiably played at Harvard, Yale, Dartmouth, Columbia, and Princeton. Oliver Wendell Holmes recalled watching base-ball at Harvard when he was an undergraduate. In 1828, the *New York Evening Post* was editorializing about the annoyance of those New York City citizens who lived around "Washington [Square] Parade, due to the large groups of men and boys playing ball and filling the air with their shouts and yells."

But as American cities grew larger and more formally organized teams came into existence in the 1830s and 1840s, negotiations concerning the rules of the game became more and more complex. Each team, naturally, insisted upon the rules that the players followed in their own practices. There is also evidence that in populous cities during the early nineteenth century some teams were organized by political parties where bitter rivalries might make impromptu agreements difficult. When teams began to be organized for competition and standings, matters of rules became much more serious. Legend insists that the Philadelphia Olympics were the first real organized team, playing as early as 1831. According to Henry Chadwick, writing in Albert G. Spalding's *Baseball Guide*, the Philadelphians gathered on a field located at the upper end of Market Street, or else at Camden fields. They had uniforms and a regular schedule, playing one day each week. The "players were laughed at [in] those days for playing ball," which was an economic waste of time according to the still-prevalent maxims of Benjamin Franklin's "The Way to Wealth." Still, sports were becoming a popular part of American culture, and the Olympics continued to compete with other Quaker City teams until 1860. Clubs sprang up everywhere. The politician Thurlow Weed claims that his base-ball team in Rochester, New York, met every afternoon during warm weather. As early as the 1840s, base-ball was extended to the Sandwich Islands by the Congregationalist missionaries who came from Connecticut to bring Christianity and Americanism to the native Hawaiians

By the 1830s or possibly sooner, the ball games fell into two basic kinds. These were eventually called "The New England Game" and the "New York

Game." The first appears to have been derived from the English game of "rounders," "run-around," or "round ball," while the second had its origins in "town-ball." Evidence gathered by Spalding shows that New Englanders knew nothing about town-ball, even as the New Yorkers knew nothing of rounders. But it seems likely that around 1850, town-ball spread into the New England states and began to replace the New England game.

Many kinds of pre-baseball games were played. The simplest resembled cricket and was called "barn ball." This was played by two players, with a barn as a backstop. After using a flat bat to hit the ball any direction whatsoever the striker would run to a base and then back to where he started, touching the barn to make a score, unless he were "soaked" (i.e., hit) or tagged by the ball before making his way back to the barn.

Another game, sometimes called "three old cat," involved three bases and an unlimited number of players. The field was triangular, and the hitters proceeded either clockwise or counterclockwise around the bases. Runners were made "out" by being hit or tagged. Balls could be struck in any direction and fielders scattered in all directions in the field.

The "rules" that governed the game called "base-ball" around the time the Philadelphia Olympics team was organized were described by the American author Robin Carver in a chapter entitled "Games with a Ball" in *The Boy's Book of Sports*. This is how he described the way base-ball was played in 1834:

> BASE, OR GOAL BALL. This game was known under a variety of names. It is sometimes called "round ball," but I believe that "base" or "goal ball" are the names generally adopted in our country. The players divide into two equal parties, and chance decides which shall have first innings. Four stones or stakes are placed from twelve to twenty yards asunder, as *a, b, c, d*, in the margin; another is put at *e*. . . .

An illustration shows a diamond formed of *a*, *b*, *c*, and *d*, with *e* set off-center, closest to *a*, much like the pitcher's mound in a modern baseball diamond.

> One of the party who is out [in the field] places himself at *e*. He tosses the ball gently toward *a*, on the right of which one of the in-party places himself, and strikes the ball, if possible, with his bat. If he miss three times, or if the ball, when struck, be caught by any of the players of the opposite side who are scattered about the field, he is out, another takes his place. If none of

these accidents take place, on striking the ball he drops the bat and runs toward b, or if he can, to c, d or even to a again. If, however, the boy who stands at e, or any of the outplayers who may happen to have the ball, strike him with it in his progress from a to b, b to c, c to d, or d to a, he is out. Supposing he can get only to b, one of his partners takes the bat, and strikes the ball in turn. If the first player can get only to c, or d, the second runs to b only, or c, as the case may be, and a third player begins; as they get home, that is, to a, they play at the ball by turns, until they get out. Then, of course, the out-players take their places.

Many particulars in this account are striking and indicate the ambiguous situation from which baseball was developed. There is no set number of players involved. The crowd that gathered to play ball, from a dozen to fifty players, would simply be divided into two teams, as generally few organized teams had yet evolved. There are no regulations concerning the distance between bases, but they are likely to be much less than ninety feet apart. The pitcher "gently" tosses the ball toward the batter, underhanded, with a stiff arm. If the batter doesn't like the pitch he may not swing. Indeed, the pitcher, according to several accounts, is likely to comply with the batter's wishes concerning the sort of pitch he wants. The pitcher places himself at no fixed distance from home, but chooses a point from which he can deliver a tossed ball to the batter's satisfaction. It is in the interest of the pitcher's team to give the batter a good ball to hit since a well-struck fly ball, if caught, might retire the side. Bases on balls are not a part of the game. Runners proceed around the bases clockwise in some locales, counterclockwise in others. There are no fixed positions and no rigid base paths. The players "scatter" around the field. A fielder might stand nearly in the batter's face and try to take the ball even as it leaves the bat, as Joseph Hooker, eventually famous as a Civil War general, said he had done as boy in the 1830s. Nor are there foul lines. Balls hit anywhere are playable. At least two catchers stand some distance in back of the batter on the chance that he might send the ball backward. There are no bases, only stakes or stones. An out is made only in three ways: the batter strikes and misses three times; an opposing player catches the batted ball on the fly, or sometimes on the first hop; finally, an out is made when a runner is struck by a ball between bases. An out cannot be made by throwing to a base ahead of a runner. The runner must be struck. This means that though the ball might have a rubber or cork center its outside had to be kept relatively soft, so that batters would not be injured when "plugged." In New York in the early nineteenth century, Charles Haswell said, the ball was fashioned "with a bit of cork, or if [the maker] were singularly fortunate, with some shreds of India rubber. Then it was wound with yarn from unraveled stockings, and some feminine member of the family covered it with patches from a soiled glove." One of Alexander Cartwright's sons recalled seeing the first ball used by Cartwright's Knickerbocker team. He described it as "about four inches in diameter and very light. . . . It was not a lively ball either." (This ball may have been used at a very early time by the Knickerbockers and saved by Alick as a historic souvenir, but it was clearly not the ball used in Knickbocker games after 1845, whose size was approximately that of the modern ball.) Long hits with soft balls were not common. Other rules follow from Carver's description. A team is retired not by three outs, but when all the batters on a side have been made out. There is no fixed number of innings, only the provision that both teams must bat around. By previous agreement the team that reaches or exceeds a certain number of runs after each team has batted once or more will become the winner. This was usually fixed somewhere between twenty and thirty runs, but a higher number could be agreed upon.

Carver's diagram appears to the modern reader to indicate that baseball was played on a diamond. This was usually not the case, though the use of the word "diamond" to describe the field occurred as early as 1838. Probably because base-ball was most often played on the village green or common, which itself was almost always rectangular in shape, the typical layout was also rectangular. The distance between home and first base, or between second and third, might be as little as twenty feet. Where the batter started from "home" on the base of the rectangle there would necessarily be a longer distance between first and second; a shorter distance at the top of the rectangle, between second and third; and the longest distance existed between third and home. With such an arrangement, many hitters reached first base, but fewer made it home.

At what point in this evolutionary process "ball" became baseball relies wholly on interpretation. What we can say, I believe, is that by the 1840s, America was ready to embrace a national game, the variety of rules in several versions of base-ball were ripe for codification, and a man who loved the game made a dramatic and lasting set of rules that was so unitary, so full of common sense, and so excellent in design that it became a solid basis on which the sport could develop. This person was Alexander Joy Cartwright Jr.

Cartwright did not pronounce, "Let there be baseball!" and bring an entirely new, freshly born entity into existence; rather, he was part of a process. Many people thought about "evolution" before Darwin formulated his theory. Others "discovered" the New World before Columbus did; Franklin was not the first to bring electricity from the skies. What we call the "American character" was not "fathered" by a single person, yet we perceive special reasons to exemplify it in Washington, Emerson, or Teddy Roosevelt. Like these, Cartwright is an eminent representative of all those anonymous figures who contributed to creating baseball. He was a distinctive consolidator. John Thorn, David Block, and Peter Morris are themselves representative of many scholars who are vigorously and helpfully teasing out the varied threads of baseball's evolution. My biography of Cartwright claims that he was a remarkably acute, inventive, and astute American and a dedicated student of the evolution of ball games and that as a leading member of the most important baseball team between 1842 and 1860, he did set down rules for baseball, by-laws for an organized team, suggestions as to a workable shape for a field, and proposals for the number and positions of the players to be involved. We know that several of his own teammates credited him with these and other codifications. We also have evidence that he participated in the founding of baseball on the West Coast, along with other transplanted Knickerbocker players. We know with certainty that he influenced and promoted the development of baseball in Hawaii, among both the upper classes and also the multiethnic workers on the plantations. Did he "invent" baseball? "Father" baseball? "Codify" or "promote" various streams from ballgames? He did a little of each. But his central claim for being singled out in baseball history is that he appeared at a certain crucial time in the "making" of the game and through his keen organizing ability he clarified the game and continued to be involved with its development. Perhaps Szymanski and Zimbalist say it best when they claim that "Cartwright . . . supplied the first unifying basis for the games that previously had been played under different rules in each community." So I conclude with them and with James C. Roberts, that "if the title, 'the father of baseball' belongs to anyone, it is Alexander J. Cartwright . . . [who] reworked the various rules of existing ballgames to produce a game that was closely akin to the version played today."

NOTES AND REFERENCES

I n this references section only two abbreviations are used: "AJC" for Alexander Joy Cartwright Jr., and HoF for the National Baseball Hall of Fame Library. Unless otherwise indicated, letters by AJC and records of the Hawaii Privy Council, the Department of Interior, and other state manuscripts are referred to in the Archives of the State of Hawaii, Honolulu, Hawaii. In what follows, sources are keyed to italicized catch phrases in the text.

THE BIRTH OF THE FATHER

Was born: AJC to Louis Lucy, April 27, 1875. *Cartwright's ancestors*: Harold Peterson, *The Man Who Invented Baseball* (New York: Scribner's, 1973), 92–96, 187. *his whole estate*: Estate of Alexander Joy Cartwright Sr., Executor Benj. C. Cartwright and W. Dubrow, distributed equally between his surviving children, Benjamin, Catherine, Alexander Jr., Alfred, and Esther, September 5, 1871, and May 30, 1872, HoF. *Peter De-Witt*: Angus Macfarlane, "The Knickerbockers: San Francisco's First Baseball Club?" *Baseball: A Journal of the Early Game* 1, no. 1 (Spring 2007): 12. *AJC's residences*: Eric Enders, Research Department, compiled July 28, 1989, HoF.

THE DREAM

about half of them: Jerry R. Erikson, "Alexander Joy Cartwright," *Royal Arch Mason Magazine* (Fall 1962): 1. *1845, he and Alfred*: Bob Hogue, "The Father of Baseball," *Hawaiian Magazine* 13, no. 3 (June 1996): 96. *Daniel Adams later recalled*: *Sporting News*, February 29, 1876; Dean A. Sullivan, *Early Innings: A Documentary History of Baseball, 1825–1908* (Lincoln: University of Nebraska Press, 1995), 14. *in 1887, William Wheaton*: Randall Brown, "How Baseball Began," *The National Pastime* 24 (2002): 51–54. *Duncan F. Curry*: "Mr. Curry's Statement," Abraham Mills Commission, clipping in HoF. *George Wright*: Mills file, vol. 1, November 15, 1904, HoF. *fifty-cent penalty*: *By-Laws and Rules of the Knickerbockers Base Ball Club*, Article V

(New York: Witt B. Smith, 1845). *Harold Seymour: Baseball: The Early Years* (New York: Oxford University Press), 15. *William Cauldwell*: Cauldwell to James Sullivan, Spalding Scrapbooks, February 11, 1905, HoF. *Charles Deborst*: AJC to Charles Deborst, in Chimpei P. Goto, "The Early Baseball in Hawaii," 774, AJC file, Japanese-American Cultural Center of Hawaii (Honolulu). *Frank Borsky*: Press Release of the Community Development Agency of Hoboken, N.J., HoF. *In 1947, Alick's*: S. F. Furukawa, "Originator of Organized Baseball," *Paradise of the Pacific* 59, no. 5 (May 1947). *Adams played shortstop*: "On Baseball When the Game Was Very New," *New York Times*, April 13, 1980, clipping in HoF. *accounting and records*: Edward Vidmer, *New York Times*, October 4, 1990; Dan Cisco, "Baseball," in *Hawai'i Sports: History, Facts, and Statistics* (Honolulu: University of Hawaii Press, 1999), 3. *one historian*: Jack Selzer, *Baseball in the Nineteenth Century: An Overview* (New York: Society for American Baseball Research, 1986). *this historic match*: Frank Borsky, Press Release of the Community Development Agency, Hoboken, N.J., 4, HoF. *Jerry Erikson*, Erikson, "Alexander Joy Cartwright," 2. *William A. Mann*: "The Elysian Fields of Hoboken, New Jersey," *Baseball* 1, no.1 (Spring 2007): 98. *Walt Whitman*: quoted in John Thorn, et al., *Total Baseball*, 6th ed. (New York: Total Sports, 1999), 499. *"it has doubtless"*: John Montgomery Ward, *Base-ball: How to Be a Player* (1888; Cleveland, Ohio: Society for American Baseball Research, 1993), 21. *Spalding's tour*: Mark Lamster, *Spalding's World Tour: The Epic Adventure That Took Baseball Around the Globe and Made It America's Game* (New York: Public Affairs, 2006).

CARTWRIGHT, DREAMING AGAIN

The news that gold: Ralph S. Kuykendall, *The Hawaiian Kingdom* (Honolulu: University of Hawaii Press), 1:319. *the California Trail*: Ralph P. Bieber, ed., *Southern Trails to California* (Glendale, Calif.: Arthur H. Clark, 1937), 51–56, 67–100, 116–25. *Alick's passport*: AJC file, February 23, 1849, HoF. *Russell had a distinguished*: E. N. Feltskog, ed., *The Oregon Trail* (Madison: University of Wisconsin Press, 1969), 552–5. *hunting and fishing*: *The Pony Express*, October 1966, clipping, HoF.

ACROSS THE PLAINS

Cartwright began his journey: AJC, *Journal of a Trip Across the Plains from Independence to San Francisco—Via Southpass Rocky Mountains of the Sierra Nevada* (1849), Bishop Museum Archives, Honolulu, Hawaii. *taught people to play*: Harold Peterson, *The Man Who Invented Baseball* (New York: Scribner's, 1973), 121. *whenever they rested*: Bruce Cartwright Jr. to John A. Hamilton, July 12, 1938.

VISIONS AND REVISIONS

buying mines: *Pacific Commercial Record* 26, no. 3122 (May 1, 1892). *Alick arrived here*: Jesse Bowman, "Alexander Cartwright's Encore," *Commercial Record* 12, no. 3 (September 1, 1977): 59. *"between diggings"*: Joseph Theroux, "Father of Baseball," *Honolulu* 26, no. 11 (May 1992): 31. *Kuykendall*: Ralph S. Kuykendall, *The Hawaiian Kingdom* (Honolulu: University of Hawaii Press), 1:132. *"There is gold"*: Letter of "Rusticus," *Polynesian*, November 24, 1849, 1. *The legend*: "Father of Local Resident was Baseball's Father," *Honolulu Advertiser*, October 20, 1919, clipping in HoF.

PARADISE BOUND

But he did play a part: Angus Macfarlane, "The Knickerbockers: San Francisco's First Baseball Club?" *Baseball: A Journal of the Early Game* 1, no. 1 (Spring 2007): 12–13. *"to the 'manor born'"*: ibid., 10. *a daguerreotype*: "The Golden West," Portsmouth Square in San Francisco January 1851, on back cover of *Base Ball: A Journal of the Early Game* 1, no. 1 (Spring 2007). *by way of China*: Alexander Bowman, *Pacific Commercial Record* 26, no. 3122 (May 1, 1892). *continuing bouts of dysentery*: William A. Borst, 1975, © United Features Syndicate, clipping, HoF.

PARADISE FOUND

A. B. Howe: Gene Wilhelm, "The Cartwright Story," *Honolulu Star Bulletin*, May 29, 1954, 4. *shipping foodstuffs*: Jesse Bowman, "Alexander Cartwright's Encore," *Commercial Record* 12, no. 3 (September 1, 1977): 60. *"sell at public auction"*: Minister of Interior to A. B. Howe, Interior Department file, June 25, 1851, B4, p. 31. *"the potato district"*: Ralph S. Kuykendall, *The Hawaiian Kingdom* (Honolulu: University of Hawaii Press), 1:313. *True, he expected*: *Pacific Commercial Advertiser* 16, no. 3422 (July 13, 1892).

THE LAST GASP OF THE GREAT SAILING SHIPS

departure of the Samuel Russell: AJC, *Journal of a Voyage from San Francisco to Sandwich Islands* (1850), Bishop Museum Archives.

MISSIONARY BASEBALL

When Cartwright relocated: Ralph S. Kuykendall, *The Hawaiian Kingdom* (Honolulu: University of Hawaii Press), 1:319. *on the bark* Yankee: Joseph Theroux, "Father of Baseball," *Honolulu* 26, no. 11 (May 1992): 31. *to bring Christianity*: Rowland B. Dodge, "What Hawaii Owes to the Missionaries," *Mid-Pacific Magazine* 12 (November 1916). *The first contingent*: *Missionary Album* (Honolulu: Hawaiian Mission Children's Society, 1909), 3. *Kuykendall writes*: Kuykendall, *The Hawaiian Kingdom*, 1:100. *"a civilizing agency"*: Kuykendall, *The Hawaiian Kingdom*, 1:101. *founded schools*: *Instructions of the Prudential Committee of the American Board of Commissions for Foreign Missions to the Sandwich Islands* (Lahainaluna, Hawaii, 1938), 27–28; Kuykendall, *The Hawaiian Kingdom*, 1:122. *their own ball games*: W. D. Westervelt, "Old Hawaiian Games in Honolulu," *Mid-Pacific Magazine* 12, no. 4 (1927): 347. *Baseball and Christ*: Mary C. Alexander and Charlotte P. Dodge, *Punahou, 1841–1941* (Berkeley: University of California Press, 1941), 117; William R. Castle, *Reminiscences* (Honolulu: Advertiser Publishing, 1960), 51. *"Many of [our children]"*: Alexander and Dodge, *Punahou*, 7. *"Shepherd of Israel"*: *Missionary Album*, 4. *Some better solution*: Alexander and Dodge, *Punahou*, 6, 2, 42. *baseball be part*: Frank Andolino, "Missionaries, Cartwright, and Spalding," *Nine: A Journal of Baseball History and Culture* 10, no. 2 (Spring 2002): 27–45. *C. P. Goto claims*: Goto, "The Early Baseball in Hawaii," 774, AJC file, Japanese-American Cultural Center of Hawaii (Honolulu). *Cisco writes*: Dan Cisco, "Baseball," in *Hawai'i Sports: History, Facts, and Statistics* (Honolulu: University of Hawaii Press, 1999), 1–2. *Goto writes*: Quoted in Richard Gina, "National Heritage Has Rich Heritage in the Territory," *Star Bulletin*, July 15, 1948, 13. *Frank Boardman*: Robert C. Schmitt, "Some Firsts in Island Leisure, *The Hawaiian Journal of History* 12 (1978): 78. *S. F. Furukawa*: Furukawa, "Originator of Organized Baseball," *Paradise of the Pacific* 59, no. 5 (May 1947). *Albert Brown Lyons*: Schmitt, "Some Firsts," 79. *In 1860*: Cisco, "Baseball," 2. *The fault seems*: Samuel C. Damon to William DeWitt Alexander, November 1859. *The first historian*: Goto, "The Early Baseball in Hawaii," 773. *Orramel Gulick*: Alexander and Dodge, *Punahou*, 117–18, 198. *Baseball had become*: Edwin North McClellan, "Baseball in Hawaii," *Forecast* (Outrigger Canoe Club) 13, no. 9 (September 1854): 8, 22.

STARTING ALL OVER AGAIN: IT'S GONNA BE ROUGH— BUT WE'RE GONNA MAKE IT

Alick set out: Joseph Theroux, "Father of Baseball," *Honolulu* 26, no. 11 (May 1992): 31. *whaling stops in Lahaina*: Ralph S. Kuykendall, *The Hawaiian Kingdom* (Honolulu: University of Hawaii Press), 1:30–39. *Bowlin was offered*: *Saturday Press*, February 1850, 1. *Privy Council*: Records of Privy Council, vol. 3B, p. 523, vol. 6B, October 7, 1851. *Together they opened*: *Saturday Press*, 1882, 1. *Coady's had*: AJC to William F. Dow, January 18, 1859.

THE NEW FIRE CHIEF ·

As a historian: H. A. Smith, "The Fire Department of the City of Honolulu," unpublished MS, 2. *without further delay*: Bob Hogue, "The Father of Baseball," *Hawaii Magazine* (June 1996): 95. *to fill the said office*: "Residents Recommending A. J. Cartwright as Chief Engineer," 4-01-7 F.O. + Ex numbered documents, Archives. *"the department flourished"*: Smith, "The Fire Department," 2; Jesse Bowman, "Alexander Cartwright's Encore," *Commercial Record* 12, no. 3 (September 1, 1977): 57. *would permit*: undated newspaper clipping, M-36 1807-56, *By April*: Interior Department Miscellaneous, May 12, 1853. *a leather hose*: S. Spencer to AJC, March 13, 1858, Interior Department Letter file. *As H. A. Smith*: Smith, "The Fire Department," 3. *The fire stations*: ibid. *Its meetings were held*: *Hawaiian Gazette*, April 2, 1889, 2.

FREEMASONRY COMES TO HAWAII

Chamber of Commerce: Erikson, "Alexander Joy Cartwright," 5. *Masonic regalia*: Privy Council Archives, 7:119, March 7, 1853. *Cartwright appealed*: September 2, 1862. *Masonic Medals*: AJC to S. K. Harzfeld, August 25, 1883.

A GIFT FROM THE SEA—AND A LOSS

"My dear old Kate": AJC to Catherine Cassio, n.d. [1852]. *epidemic in Honolulu*: Archives, June 15, 1853.

BACK TO BASEBALL

"Honolulu is one": Harold Peterson, *The Man Who Invented Baseball* (New York: Scribner's, 1973), 111. *Peterson writes*: *The Man Who Invented Baseball*, 172–73. *"Many an hour"*: Dan Cisco, "Baseball," in *Hawai'i Sports: History, Facts, and Statistics* (Honolulu: University of Hawaii Press, 1999), 2. *A student at Punahou*: William R. Castle, *Reminiscences* (Honolulu: Advertiser Publishing, 1960).

DEWITT AND HIS BROTHERS

Writing to Hemenway: AJC to Hemenway July 25, 1856. *he must be punctilious*: AJC to DeWitt Cartwright, July 26, 1856. *In subsequent letters*: AJC to DeWitt Cartwright, August 27, 1857. *"Please write me"*: AJC to George D. Cassio, May 1, 1856; AJC to Catherine and George D. Cassio, July 26, 1856. *To George*: AJC to George D. Cassio, August 16, 1853. *Before the arrival*: Goto, "The Early Baseball in Hawaii," 774, AJC file, Japanese-American Cultural Center of Hawaii (Honolulu). *This one-story, cot-*

tage-style house: AJC to George D. Cassio, March 1, 1856; Thomas Thrum, "Honolulu Sixty Years Ago," *Hawaiian Annual* (Honolulu: n.p., 1905), 44. *"How much I wish"*: AJC to Thomas Shillabee, June 15, 1853. *He wrote*: AJC to Richard I. Howland, January 22, 1872. *go to Philadelphia*: AJC to Read & Co., September 2, 1873. *prepared "to celebrate"*: AJC to Bruce Cartwright, June 20, 1876. *Alfred's Honolulu venture*: AJC to James Lee Edgar, March 28, 1854. *Alick lent him*: AJC to George D. Cassio, May 1, 1856, March 5, 1856. *Alick wrote back*: AJC to Alfred Cartwright, March 5, 1856. *"Alfred has just"* : AJC to George D. Cassio, 1856. *Alick told Kate*: AJC to Catherine Cassio November 29, 1883. *"I hold the agency"*: AJC to Alfred Cartwright, March 10, 1883. *"the old ones"*: AJC to Read & Co., September 2, 1873.

CARTWRIGHT & CO., LTD.

Association of Cold Springs: *Pacific Commercial Advertiser* 16, no. 3422 (July 13, 1892): 1. *"I have been most fortunate"*: AJC to Capt. William H. Vinal, May 1, 1856. *"I am not ambitious"*: AJC to Capt. William H. Vinal, July 2, 1856. *asked a relative*: AJC to George D. Cassio, July 26, 1856. *"a thousand details"*: AJC to Catherine Cassio, September 28, 1883.

ALEXANDER JOY CARTWRIGHT JR., AMERICAN

"So strong" : *Pacific Commercial Advertiser* 16, no. 3422 (July 13, 1892): 13. *"my beloved country"*: AJC to R. H. Van Brunt, April 30, 1873. *"I still think"*: AJC to Mr. Muir, 1857. *American Relief Fund*: *Pacific Commercial Advertiser* 16, no. 3422 (July 13, 1892): 13. *its first treasurer*: E. F. O'Halloran to AJC, February 15, 1857. *to his son*: AJC to Bruce Cartwright, December 18, 1873. *"Kalakaua"*: AJC to Catherine Cassio, November 15, 1881. *William H. Seward*: AJC to Secretary of State William H. Seward, December 1, 1866. *Cartwright complained*: AJC to W. C. Ralston, December 5, 1877; AJC to J. C. Spalding January 22, 1872. *"Mr. Cartwright has often"*: *Pacific Commercial Advertiser* 16, no. 3422 (July 13, 1892): 13. *"We think it not"*: ibid., 14. *"Perhaps his most"*: ibid., 2.

THE SOCIAL WHIRL

A visitor to the city: Daniel E. Bandmann, *An Actor's Tour* (London: 1885), MS in Archives of the State of Hawaii. *Mary Groesbeck*: AJC Archives, Spalding Estate, M-36, Box 1. *"The town"*: AJC to Edwin Putnam, August 23, 1875. *a "fine brick building"*: AJC to Alfred de Forest Cartwright, December 18, 1880. *Daniel E. Bandmann*: Bandmann, *An Actor's Tour* (London, 1885). *Alick belonged*: Archives of the State of Hawaii, small notebook, M-36 1867–74. *"Mr. Cartwright was always"*: Mary A. Burbank, "Story of the Honolulu Library and Reading Room Association," *Hawaii Historical Society Annual Reports* (1927): 20. *Father Damien*: AJC to Father Damien, sending $20, March 25, 1882; and $40, June 5, 1882. *He even turned*: *Pacific Commercial Advertiser* 16, no. 3422 (July 13, 1892): 13. *Consul for Peru*: Mariano Ignacio Prado, Presidente de la Republica del Peru, Re-Appointment of "Don Alexander J. Cartwright" as Consul, August 22, 1878.

ADVISOR TO THE QUEEN

Alick had begun: AJC Archives, Spalding Estate, M-36, #462. *Queen's Hospital*: *Charter and By-Laws of the Queen's Hospital, Honolulu* (Honolulu: Commercial Advertiser Co., 1859). *for four years*: R. G. Davis to minister of the Interior Department, December 2, 1863, Archives of Interior Department. *Rufus A. Lyman*: to AJC, January 27, 1875. *D. H. Hitchcock*: to AJC, February 21, 1875. *"I have got all"*: AJC to Paul Lahaina, August 17, 1875. *"I noticed"*: Valdemar Knudson to AJC, 1877; Tom Hayselden to AJC, March 1, 1878; F. M. Hatch to AJC, September 17, 1884. *By 1877, Alick*: W. D. Alexander to AJC, Interior Department March 8, 1877. *Interior Department documents*: Interior Department, January 1, 1885, 502. *Alick was informed*: R. A. Lyman to AJC, Interior Department, March 5, 1875. *a parcel of her land*: William R. Buchanan to AJC, conveying deed, Interior Department, April 16, 1875. *He not only spoke*: AJC, July 14, 1892. *U Moe O A. J. Kahalaeka*: HoF. *Know . . . that we*: Land Files, Interior Department Papers, December 4, 1883. *Among his papers*: AJC to Valdemar Knudson, February 24, 1880. *He guaranteed*: AJC to Esther Dubrow, 1880.

DEATHS AND NEW LIFE

"most happy": AJC to George D. Cassio, July 26, 1856. *the $200 annual*: AJC to Benjamin Cartwright, January 18, 1861, HoF. *a rare personal statement*: AJC to Dean Pullman, Oversize, September 5, 1873. *Bruce was always*: AJC to Louis C. Sartori, 1873. *St. Augustine's*: Bruce Cartwright to Rt. Rev. Bishop Winfield, September 19, 1882. *dangers of swimming*: AJC to Bruce Cartwright, August 19, 1875. *"Great God"*: AJC to Louis C. Sartori, July 29, 1872. *to play baseball*: AJC to Louis A. Arthur, July 2, 1873. *"wild days"*: AJC to AJC III, July 26, 1882. *followed his father's advice*: AJC to Bruce Cartwright, February 12, 1881. *Alick was well aware*: AJC to Alfred de Forest Cartwright, February 16, 1886. *In writing to his brother*: AJC to Alfred de Forest Cartwright, January 14, 1882. *He wrote to his namesake*: AJC to AJC III, March 10, 1882. *He rehearsed a history*: Bruce Cartwright to AJC III, July 29, 1882. *"I am sick"*: AJC to AJC III, July 26, 1882. *"be upright"*: AJC to AJC III, July 10, 1882. *Bruce urged his brother*: Bruce Cartwright to AJC III, July 29, 1882. *"a sore trial"*: AJC to Alfred de Forest Cartwright, March 17, 1882. *When Bruce and Alick*: AJC to Alfred de Forest Cartwright, March 10,

1882; Bruce Cartwright to AJC III, June 5, 1882. *Teresa called upon*: AJC to AJC III, July 25, 1882. *Alick persuaded*: AJC to Catherine Cassio, November 20, 1882. *Alick finally determined*: AJC to Alfred de Forest Cartwright, March 11, 1882. *Allie was married again*: AJC to Catherine Cassio, November 29, 1883.

KING SUGAR

The first sugar plantation: Ralph S. Kuykendall, *The Hawaiian Kingdom* (Honolulu: University of Hawaii Press), 1:175. *The author of*: Ronald T. Takaki, *Pau Hana* (Honolulu: University of Hawaii Press, 1983). *Howe was already*: Printed broadside, Judicial Papers, 1852, 6–7. *DeBow's Review, etc.*: in Takaki, *Pau Hana*, 16–17, 19. *He treated the matter*: AJC to John Always, March 1, 1876. *Later, in October*: AJC to A. P. Everett, October 24, 1876. *Cartwright confidently observed*: AJC to J. B. Berrill March 10, 1882; AJC to Elias Hempstead, June 29, 1877. *his insurance agency*: Records of Insurance on Sugar Plantations Since 1859, April 1877, 1877–83. *focused his attention*: AJC to John Cashman, Oversize, May 21, 1879. *this space*: Thomas J. Thrum, *Hawaiian Annual* (Honolulu: n.p., 1910), 43. *his brother Alfred*: AJC to Alfred de Forest Cartwright, December 18, 1880. *At a meeting of*: H. S. Pratt, secretary, Waimanolo Sugar Company, to Samuel G. Wilder, minister of the interior, oversize, May 2, 1879. *Alick insisted*: AJC to John A. Cummins, January 19, 1881, April 6, 1881. *We have a vivid*: Daniel E. Bandmann, *An Actor's Tour* (London: 1885), 10, 10a, 11, 12, 15, 4. *By 1880 Cartwright*: AJC to Elias Hempstead, November 16, 1880. *"Keep a variety"*: Takaki, *Pau Hana*, 24. *remarked to Elias Hempstead*: AJC to Elias Hempstead, June 29, 1880.

BASEBALL ON THE PLANTATIONS

"Baseball had several": MacKinnon Simpson and John Brizdle, *Streetcar Days in Honolulu* (Honolulu: JLB Press), 92. *In contrast to gambling, etc.*: Ronald T. Takaki, *Pau Hana* (Honolulu: University of Hawaii Press, 1983), 103, 105. *William R. Castle remembered*: Castle, "The Introduction of Baseball," *The Friend* (March 1924): 70. *As one writer*: Exhibit on Baseball, Japanese-American Cultural Center of Hawaii, 1999. *Chinese baseball*: Oral Interviews on Baseball, M6, p. 7, Japanese-American Cultural Center of Hawaii; Michael M. Okihiro, *AJA Baseball in Hawaii: Ethnic Pride and Tradition* (Honolulu: Hawaii Hochi, 1999). *"Punahou Athletic Club"*: *Punahou Reporter*, May 27, 1875, section 1, p. 4. *The minutes of*: Arthur Alexander, "Baseball at Punahou Thirty-Seven Years Ago," *Oahuan* (June 1906): 25–27. *His daughter Mary*: Harold Peterson, *The Man Who Invented Baseball* (New York: Scribner's, 1973), 188. *While few of the farmers*: Jill Tanioka, "Besuboro: A Reflection on Japanese Culture," MS in Japanese-American Cultural Center of Hawaii.

SPALDING'S WORLD TOUR—FIRST STOP, HAWAII

Albert G. Spalding: Mark Lamster, *Spalding's World Tour: The Epic Adventure That Took Baseball Around the Globe and Made It America's Game* (New York: Public Affairs, 2006), 18–23. *It occurred to me*: Spalding, *America's National Game* (1911; reprint, Lincoln: University of Nebraska Press, 1992), 175–76. *Grover Cleveland*: Lamster, *Spalding's World Tour*, 54–5. *Helen Dauvray*: Henry Clay Palmer, "Mrs. Ward's Good Taste," *Sporting News*, 1888; Lamster, *Spalding's World Tour*, 50. *A game was scheduled*: Henry Clay Palmer, *Athletic Sports in America* (Philadelphia: Hubbard Brothers, 1889), 708, 721. *They found the Honolulu diamond*: "Received by a King," Tommy Burns Scrapbook, November 25, 1888, HoF. *"a picked nine"*: *Hawaiian Annual for 1890* (Honolulu: Steam Front, 1889), 101. *The local Punahou A.C.*: Dan McGuire, "Early Baseball Days," *Honolulu Advertiser* (1888): 5–6, 79. *escorted to the Iolani Palace*: "Arrangement for the Reception of the Ball-Players and Games," *Daily Bulletin*, November 31, 1888, 3. *"We found"*: Palmer, *Athletic Sports*, 451. *"Baseball, he wrote"*: Spalding, "In the Field Papers: Baseball," *Cosmopolitan* (October 1887): 604–10. *Spalding later recalled*: Lamster, *Spalding's World Tour*, 53, 107. *"The town is"*: Walter Francis Friar, "Mark Twain's Prose Poem on Hawaii—and Baseball," 96. *"Kalakaua," Lamster writes*: Lamster, *Spalding's World Tour*, 107. *In 1904, the year*: Spalding, "The Origin and Early History of Baseball," typed manuscript, 2, HoF, reprinted in *The American Boy* (May 1905): 215. *A year later, in 1905*: "Baseball as It Has Been Played/History of the Popular Game," *San Diego Evening Tribune*, April 1905, undated clipping, HoF. *In his 1911 book*: Spalding, *America's National Game*, 46. *"barbaric plenty"*: Lamster, *Spalding's World Tour*, 111. *All of us knew*: John Montgomery Ward, "Poi With King Kalakaua," Tommy Burns Scrapbooks, HoF. *"like an oriental"*: AJC to Bertha Turnbull, August 19, 1880. *Ward told the readers*: "Ward's Pacific Letters," quoted in Lamster, *Spalding's World Tour*, 113. *Cap Anson*: "Diary of the Cap'n Anson," quoted in Lamster, *Spalding's World Tour*, 113. *As the* Alameda: John Montgomery Ward, "The Big Nine in Honolulu," 1888, Tommy Burns Scrapbooks, HoF. *Twain . . . Depew*: Friar, "Mark Twain's Prose Poem." *For the baseball enthusiasts*: *Hawaiian Almanac and Annual for 1890*, 101.

THE FINAL DISSOLVING

1873 marks the first: AJC to Dean Pullman, September 5, 1873. *A little later*: AJC to Thomas H. Holborn, n.d. *Alick confided*: AJC to Esther Dubrow, April 10, 1881. *He told his sister Kate*: AJC to Catherine Cassio, December 19, 1879. *For years afterward*: AJC to Alfred de Forest Cartwright, June 5, 1882. *Alexander Cartwright bought*: Robert E. Van Dyke, "Alexander Joy Cartwright," *Coins* 8 (October 1964): 24. *As reported in a native*: *Ka Leo O Ka Lahui*, 1892, translated by Esther Mookini, HoF. *"No man in this city"*: *Pacific Commercial Advertiser* 16, no. 3422 (July 13, 1892): 1–2. *Alick made a will*: "Last Will and Testament of Alexander Joy Cartwright," Archives of the State of Hawaii, Docket #2607, vol. 8, p. 116; vol. 17, p. 8, M-24, folder 4. *The beneficiaries of the will*: Probate documents in Probate Court, February 15, 1893.

CARTWRIGHT'S SECOND LIFE: MYTH INTO HISTORY

Ward wrote to Spalding: quoted in Dean A. Sullivan, *Early Innings: A Documentary History of Baseball, 1825–1908* (Lincoln: University of Nebraska Press, 1995), 293. *Spalding outlined his theory*: Spalding Scrapbooks, HoF. *But Wheaton's memory*: John Thorn, "Four Fathers of Baseball," http://thornpricks.blogspot.com/2005_07_01_archive.html July 16, 2005. *a witness named Albert Graves*: Spalding Scrapbooks, HoF. *At first he wrote cautiously*: Spalding Scrapbooks, HoF. *Mr. Pratt*: Spalding to Pratt, August 16, 1905. *But this was at least*: Thorn, "Four Fathers of Baseball." *So, in the end*: Stefan Szymanski and Andrew Zimbalist, *National Pastime: How Americans Play Baseball and the Rest of the World Plays Soccer* (Washington, D.C.: Brookings Institution Press, 2005), 16. *But Graves's "evidence"*: Harold Peterson, *The Man Who Invented Baseball* (New York: Scribner's, 1973), 180–83. *Robert Smith, author*: Joseph Theroux, "Father of Baseball," *Honolulu* 26, no. 11 (May 1992): 30. *Many people began to believe*: quoted in Joel Zoss and John Bowman, *Diamonds in the Rough: The Untold History of Baseball* (New York: Contemporary Books, 1996), 47. *An All-Star team*: *Honolulu Advertiser*, January 24, 1923, with photos; "A Tribute, to the Father of Baseball," *San Francisco Call and Post*, January 31, 1923. *At Ebbets Field*: August 31, 1939, clipping in HoF. *Elysian Field*: *Oneonta Star*, June 22, 1992; "Hoboken Fete to Tell 'Real' Baseball Story," *Hoboken Star Ledger*, June 1990, clippings in HoF.

APPENDIX 2: DID CARTWRIGHT "REALLY INVENT" BASEBALL?

Governor William Bradford: Bradford, *Of Plymouth Plantation, 1620–1647* (New York: Knopf, 1963) , 97, 46. *"Base ball or 'balle aux bases'"*: "Les Champions Américaines à Paris," *Le Temps*, March 5, 1889. *Our earliest president*: John C. Fitzpatrick, ed., *The Writings of George Washington from the Original Manuscript Sources, 1745–1799* (Washington, D.C.: United States Printing Office, 1934), 11:348, citing *Military Journal of George Ewing* (Yonkers, N.Y.: Privately printed, 1928). *The earliest mention*: John Thorn, *The Berkshire Eagle*, May 12, 2004; Thorn, "1791 and All That: Baseball and the Berkshires," *Base Ball: A Journal of the Early Game* 1, no. 1 (Spring 2007): 119–126. *Thomas Jefferson*: *Albany Sunday Times Union*, October 13, 1991, clipping in HoF. *A child's primer*: John Newberry, *A Little Pretty Pocket Book* (London: 1744); illustrated in Thorn, "1791 and All That." *Mary Lipell*: *New York Times*, November 2, 1890. *Jane Austen*: *Northanger Abbey* (1796; New York: E. P. Dutton, 1950), 3. *Horatio Smith*:

Harold Peterson, *The Man Who Invented Baseball* (New York: Scribner's, 1973), 14, 10, 11. *"players were laughed at"*: Mills Commission file, Spalding Scrapbooks, HoF. *Robin Carver: The Boy's Book of Sports* (1838), in file on "History of Baseball," HoF. *Joseph Hooker*, Peterson, pp. 10, 11. *Szymanski*: Szymanski and Zimbalist, National *Pastime*, p. 16. *James C. Roberts: Hardball on the Hill: Baseball Stories from Our Nation's Capital* (Chicago: Triumph Books, 2001), 33.

ACKNOWLEDGMENTS

....

This book could not have been written without the invaluable assistance of the curators and staffs of the Archives of the State of Hawaii; the Special Collections Library of the University of Hawaii, Manoa; De Soto Brown and the staff of the Library and Manuscript Collections of the Bishop Museum; the Hawaii Historical Society and Reading Room; the Collections of the Japanese-American Cultural Center; the Filipino-American Center; and the State Library of Hawaii—all located in Honolulu.

Claudette Burke and the staff of the Library of the National Baseball Hall of Fame in Cooperstown, N.Y., provided a warm atmosphere and expert research assistance.

For generous assistance in helping me to get and choose photos, I am grateful to Ju Sun Yi of the Hawaii State Archives; Jenny Ambrose of the National Baseball Hall of Fame; Cynthia Engle of the Bishop Museum; and Mark Rucker of Transcendental Graphics.

I was significantly aided by my three research assistants: Hillary Bunsow, Jennifer Jared, and Chad Jimenez.

Professor Samuel Yamashita of Pomona College first interested me in the topic of baseball in Hawaii. Jim Charlton, at the Society of American Baseball Research, was ever gracious in his advice and encouragement.

Professor Ronald Gottesman and an anonymous reader gave me excellent guidance in my final revisions.

My editor, Peter Dimock, was enthusiastic from the first about this biography. Kabir Dandona was helpful in many gracious ways, especially in establishing the credits for the photographs and for the connections he always kept between the Press and me. Michael Haskell is the finest manuscript and production editor with whom I have worked.

Finally, as always, my wife, Helen, showered me with the inspiration and more than enough love and happy energy to help me bring this project to a conclusion.

INDEX